THE NEW NATION

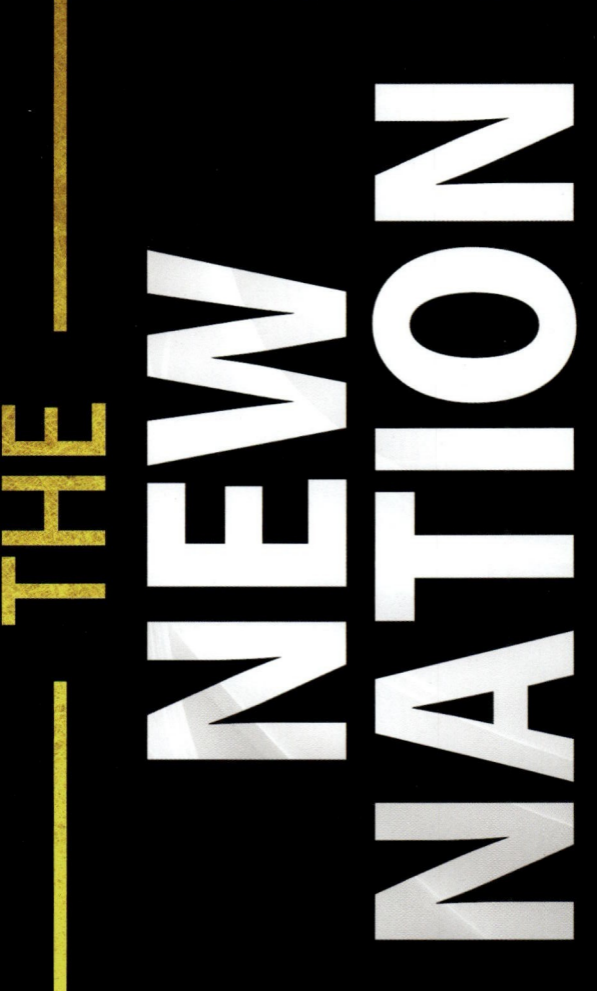

… EARLY AMERICAN HISTORY …

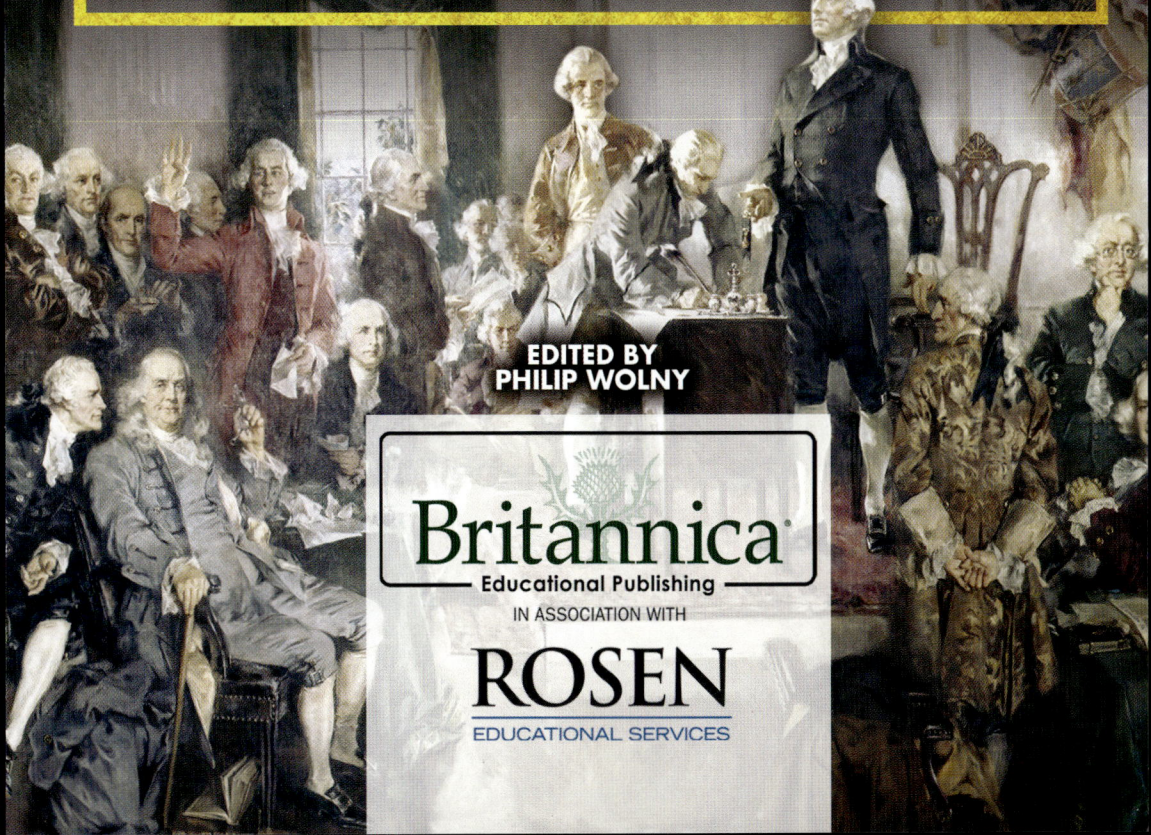

THE NEW NATION

EDITED BY
PHILIP WOLNY

Britannica
Educational Publishing

IN ASSOCIATION WITH

ROSEN
EDUCATIONAL SERVICES

Allen County Public Library

Published in 2016 by Britannica Educational Publishing (a trademark of Encyclopædia Britannica, Inc.) in association with The Rosen Publishing Group, Inc.
29 East 21st Street, New York, NY 10010

Copyright © 2016 by Encyclopædia Britannica, Inc. Britannica, Encyclopædia Britannica, and the Thistle logo are registered trademarks of Encyclopædia Britannica, Inc. All rights reserved.

Rosen Publishing materials copyright © 2016 The Rosen Publishing Group, Inc. All rights reserved

Distributed exclusively by Rosen Publishing.
To see additional Britannica Educational Publishing titles, go to rosenpublishing.com.

First Edition

Britannica Educational Publishing
J.E. Luebering: Director, Core Reference Group
Anthony L. Green: Editor, Compton's by Britannica

Rosen Publishing
John Kemmerer: Editorial Director
Philip Wolny: Editor
Nelson Sá: Art Director
Michael Moy: Designer
Cindy Reiman: Photography Manager
Philip Wolny: Photo Researcher

Library of Congress Cataloging-in-Publication Data

Names: Wolny, Philip, editor.
Title: The new nation / edited by Philip Wolny.
Description: First edition. | New York : Britannica Educational Publishing in association with Rosen Educational Services, 2016. | Series: Early American history | Includes bibliographical references and index. | Audience: Grades 7-12.
Identifiers: LCCN 2015040968 | ISBN 9781680482706 (library bound)
Subjects: LCSH: United States--History--1783-1865--Juvenile literature.
Classification: LCC E301 .N49 2016 | DDC 973--dc23
LC record available at http://lccn.loc.gov/2015040968

Manufactured in the United States of America

Photo Credits: Cover, p. 3 Architect of the Capitol; pp. 7, 11, 44-45 Everett Historical/Shutterstock.com; p. 9, 34 Kean Collection/Archive Photos/Getty Images; p. 13 Buyenlarge/Archive Photos/Getty Images; p. 15 © 2015 Encyclopædia Britannica, Inc.; pp. 20, 32 SuperStock/Getty Images; pp. 22-23 Driendl Group/Photolibrary/Getty Images; p. 25 Stock Montage/Archive Photos/Getty Images; pp. 27, 51 Private Collection/Bridgeman Images; p. 33 Library of Congress Prints and Photographs Division; pp. 36- 37, 38-39 © North Wind Picture Archives/Alamy; pp. 40-41 Universal History Archives/Universal Images Group/Getty Images; p. 46 FPG/The Image Bank/Getty Images; p. 49 Encyclopaedia Britannica/Universal Images Group/Getty Images; p. 53 Photo Researchers/Science Source/Getty Images; pp. 54-55 Hulton Archive/Getty Images; p. 60 Kim Grant/Lonely Planet Images/Getty Images; pp. 62-63 De Agostini Picture Library/Getty Images; p. 65 Library Company of Philadelphia, PA, USA/Bridgeman Images

CONTENTS

INTRODUCTION 6

CHAPTER ONE
A NEW NATION ARISES 9

CHAPTER TWO
A STRONGER, UNITED REPUBLIC 19

CHAPTER THREE
**NEW CHALLENGES: THE REPUBLIC
ENTERS THE 19TH CENTURY** 31

CHAPTER FOUR
**THE COMPLICATED LEGACY OF
WESTERN EXPANSION** 47

CHAPTER FIVE
A NEW AND CHANGING AMERICA 58

CONCLUSION 69
TIMELINE 71
GLOSSARY 73
FOR MORE INFORMATION 75
BIBLIOGRAPHY 78
INDEX 79

INTRODUCTION

In 1783 the American Revolution was finally over. America's victory over Great Britain ended the colonial period and brought independence to the United States. The new nation was still a confederation of states with a weak central government under a makeshift constitution, the Articles of Confederation. Its population of about 4 million largely resided in the countryside. A major economic depression was underway, and its people were still figuring out how to run their own affairs without British control.

Within a few short decades, the nation would expand significantly in size, population, and economic power. Its new Constitution, the able stewardship of its leaders, and the efforts of its everyday people would be instrumental in its rise during the 19th century. This rapid development would not be easy, however.

The time after the American Revolution was one of instability and change. The lack of a strong central authority made the new nation only a league of loosely tied states that were virtually independent. The national government could not collect taxes, regulate commerce, or settle disputes among the states. Its work was further handicapped by the people's lack of feeling for national unity. Most Americans still owed their first loyalties to their home state.

INTRODUCTION

From the struggles of the American Revolution—such as the tough winter at Valley Forge faced by General George Washington and his troops—the United States emerged to establish a democratic republic.

The process of creating a workable government for the new nation required both the collective wisdom of the Founding Fathers as well as some trial and error. The lessons of what the Americans had considered unfair under British rule were still fresh in their minds and strongly influenced their thinking. At the same time, they had to craft a system powerful enough to unite such a diverse nation.

The United States would also have to settle problems with Britain, France, and other foreign nations as it sought to establish its place in the world community. Careful navigation in foreign affairs was crucial in securing the country's security and economic well-being. Money and financial troubles, including problems with currency, plagued the new nation, and these too would have to be fixed.

The decisions that the Founding Fathers made in the early years of the United States, along with the industriousness and boldness of its citizens, would affect the direction and development of the nation for decades and centuries to come.

CHAPTER ONE

A NEW NATION ARISES

The United States had finally won its struggle to separate from Great Britain. The British had surrendered to General George Washington's forces at Yorktown, Virginia, on October 19, 1781, in the last major battle of the American Revolution.

The U.S. and Britain signed a preliminary peace treaty on November 30, 1782. The agreement was finalized on September 3, 1783, officially ending hostilities. Known as the Treaty of Paris, it recognized America's independence. It established the nation's boundaries as Canada on the north, the Mississippi River on the west, and Florida, which had been ceded back to Spain by Britain, on the south.

This illustration shows British and American delegates signing the Treaty of Paris.

THE ARTICLES OF CONFEDERATION: THE FIRST CONSTITUTION OF THE UNITED STATES

When the United States declared its independence in July 1776, the only institution acting as a central government was the Continental Congress. The states were operating under old colonial charters. Thus, at the same time the united colonies were fighting for independence, they were faced with the need to improvise a permanent national government and to formulate state constitutions. The states drew up and adopted their own constitutions between 1777 and 1780.

The Second Continental Congress had begun working on a plan for national government in June 1776. A committee composed of one delegate from each state presented the first draft of a national constitution on July 12, 1776 — just eight days after the Declaration of Independence was signed. Strong differences of opinion among the 13 states about a variety of issues kept debate going for more than a year before the new constitution, known as the Articles of Confederation, was submitted to the states for approval.

The first aim of the Articles was to give Congress the powers required to win the war. But the citizens realized that in peacetime they would have to continue working together. They would have to defend their frontiers and protect their trading vessels. They needed

ARTICLES

Of Confederation and perpetual Union between the States of *New-Hampshire, Massachusetts-Bay, Rhode-Island* and *Providence Plantations, Connecticut, New-York, New-Jersey, Pennsylvania, Delaware, Maryland, Virginia, North-Carolina, South-Carolina* and *Georgia.*

ARTICLE I. THE Stile of this CONFEDERACY shall be "The UNITED STATES OF AMERICA. *Stile of the Confederacy*

ART. II. EACH State retains its sovereignty, freedom and independence, and every power, jurisdiction and right, which is not by this confederation expressly delegated to the United States, in Congress assembled. *Sovereignty and Independence of the respective States.*

ART. III. THE said states hereby severally enter into a firm league of friendship with each other, for their common defence, the security of their liberties, and their mutual and general welfare, binding themselves to assist each other, against all force offered to, or attacks made upon them, or any of them, on account of religion, sovereignty, trade, or any other pretence whatever. *Design of the confederation, as it regards common security.*

ART. IV. The better to secure and perpetuate mutual friendship and intercourse among the people of the different states in this union, the free inhabitants of each of these states, paupers, vagabonds, and fugitives from justice excepted, shall be intitled to all priviledges and immunities of free citizens in the several states; and the people of each state shall have free ingress and regress to and from any other state, and shall enjoy therein all the privileges of trade and commerce, subject to the same duties, impositions and restrictions as the inhabitants thereof respectively, provided that such restriction shall not extend so far as to prevent the removal of property imported into any state, to any other state of which the owner is an inhabitant; provided also that no imposition, duties or restriction shall be laid by any state, on the property of the United States, or either of them. *Social and mutual intercourse among the States.*

IF

This is the first page of a 1777 copy of the Articles of Confederation, the first constitution of the United States. The document described this initial union of the states as a "firm league of friendship."

a common postal service and diplomats abroad. So the Articles created a perpetual union—not merely a war alliance—and declared that the name of the nation should be the United States of America.

The main problem in drafting the Articles was that of dividing the powers of government between the states and Congress. Britain had formerly supplied the navy, the postal service, the military, and the diplomatic agencies for America. Accordingly, the Articles gave Congress the power to raise and maintain an army and a navy, to make war and peace, to negotiate treaties, to fix standards of coinage and of weights and measures, and to provide a postal service.

On the other hand the patriot leaders had objected to Britain's claims that Parliament could tax the colonies, regulate their trade and currency, interfere in their local concerns, and manage relations with the Indians. Therefore the Articles did not allow Congress any control over the domestic affairs of the states. Nor could it levy taxes; it could only ask the states for funds. Congress could make commercial treaties and also superintend Indian affairs if these did not conflict with state laws.

Each of the 13 states was to have only one vote in Congress, though it might send from two to seven delegates, and nine of the 13 votes were required before Congress could act. The enforcement of all laws and the administration of justice were left to the states. The Articles could be changed only by unanimous vote of the Confederation. Any power not specifically granted to Congress was reserved to the states.

STRENGTHS AND WEAKNESSES OF CONFEDERATION

The Articles were adopted by Congress on November 15, 1777, and submitted to the states for ratification. The smaller states, especially Maryland, objected to the claims of Virginia, Massachusetts, the Carolinas, Georgia, New York, and Connecticut to the lands west of the Appalachians. Maryland felt that if these states had all the land they claimed, they might become too powerful. Only when the states with western claims agreed to turn over these lands to Congress for the use of all the states would

A 1784 map of the United States shows the 13 American colonies offset in color, in contrast to the western frontier, which would eventually be settled and split up into new states.

Maryland ratify the Articles. It finally signed them on March 1, 1781.

Thus the Articles, which had been laid before the states in 1777 and which were intended to help win the war, did not come into effect until a few months before the close of the war. The new Congress had only to keep the armies in the field until the war was won. It provided four executive offices to superintend foreign affairs, finance, war, and marine. At the end of the war, Congress negotiated the Treaty of Paris.

Congress worked out important policies with reference to the western lands ceded by the states. The Ordinance of 1785 divided these lands into townships of 36 square miles (93 square kilometers). The townships in turn were subdivided into sections of one square mile (640 acres) each. These lands were then sold at auction at a minimum price of one dollar an acre. Many settlers were able to buy farms of their own. The Ordinance of 1787, also known as the Northwest Ordinance, opened the territory to settlement and outlined the representative government later used for all the continental territories. It promised that the region should eventually be divided into new states that would enter the Union on an equal footing with the original 13.

After the American Revolution the states refused to pay taxes requested by Congress; hence the general government could not pay the public debt or even the interest on it. The navy was inadequate to

A NEW NATION ARISES

protect foreign commerce. Now that the states were out of the British Empire, they could not trade freely with England and its West Indies colonies. Western settlers needed an outlet for their produce down the Mississippi.

Spain, however, held the mouth of the river and blocked American shipping from New Orleans.

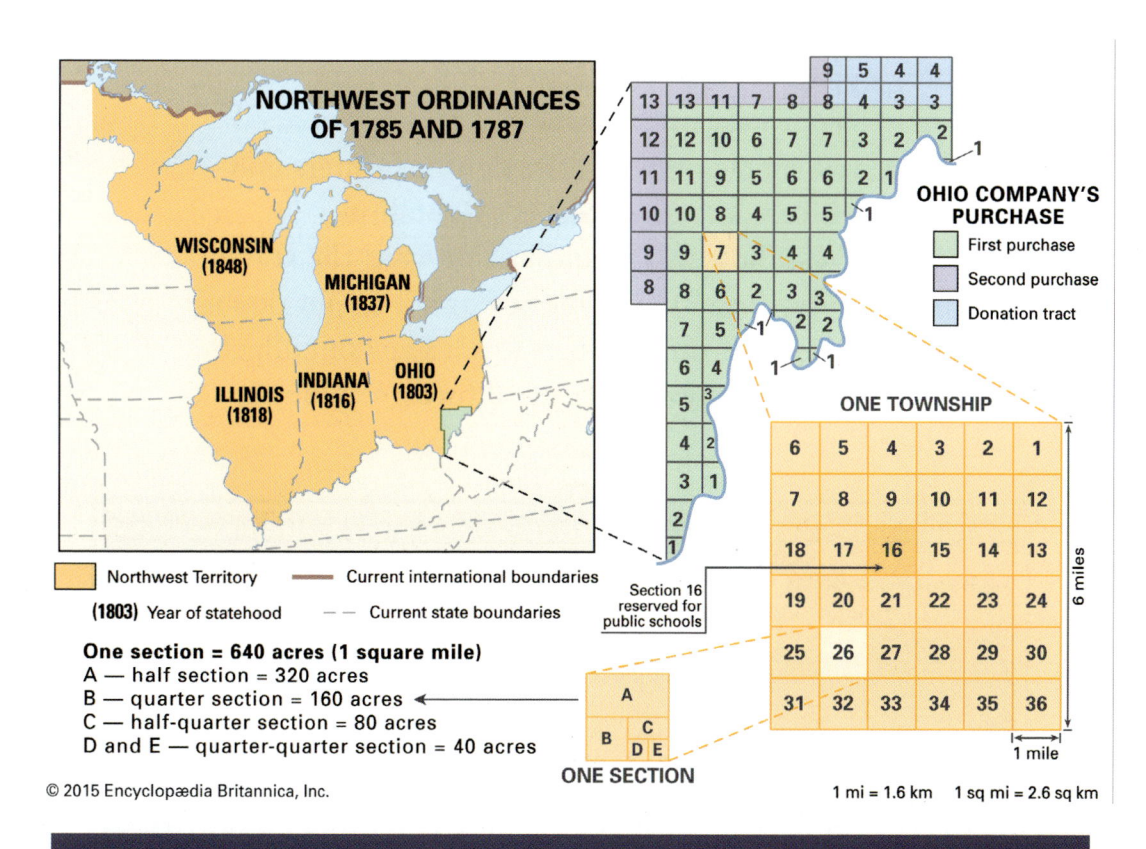

NORTHWEST ORDINANCES OF 1785 AND 1787

WISCONSIN (1848)
MICHIGAN (1837)
ILLINOIS (1818)
INDIANA (1816)
OHIO (1803)

Northwest Territory
(1803) Year of statehood
Current international boundaries
Current state boundaries

One section = 640 acres (1 square mile)
A — half section = 320 acres
B — quarter section = 160 acres
C — half-quarter section = 80 acres
D and E — quarter-quarter section = 40 acres

© 2015 Encyclopædia Britannica, Inc.

OHIO COMPANY'S PURCHASE
First purchase
Second purchase
Donation tract

ONE TOWNSHIP

Section 16 reserved for public schools

ONE SECTION

1 mi = 1.6 km   1 sq mi = 2.6 sq km

The map depicts the Northwest Territory and the five states eventually created from it. Also shown are the first land purchase, by the Ohio Company of Associates, and the method of dividing the land into townships.

Congress found that it could not get commercial favors from either Britain or Spain. Because the states had the final say in commercial regulations, a treaty of Congress had little force and the European countries preferred to deal separately with the states.

After the Revolution a period of hard times set in. The price of farm products was very low, and the farmers bought manufactured goods on credit, which they found difficult to pay back. They soon asked their legislatures to issue paper money that creditors would have to accept. Massachusetts experienced a violent struggle between the debtor farmers and their creditors known as Shays's Rebellion.

Congress, however, could not prevent the states from issuing cheap paper money or act to put down a civil war. It was unable to enforce a law or collect a tax. It had no power to control foreign trade or

SHAYS'S REBELLION: ECONOMIC UNREST ERUPTS

After the American Revolution the young nation was torn by unsettled economic conditions and a severe depression. Paper money was in circulation, but little of it was honored at face value. Merchants and other "sound money" men wanted currencies with gold

backing. In Massachusetts the "sound money" men ran the government. Most of those who were harmed by the depression had no property and were thus unable to vote. The quarrel grew until thousands of men in the western counties rose in armed revolt. They were led by Daniel Shays (1747?-1825), who had been a captain during the American Revolution. Shays's Rebellion lasted from August 1786 to February 1787.

The agitators objected to heavy land and poll taxes, the high cost of lawsuits, high salaries of state officials, oppressive court decisions, and dictatorial rulings of the state senate. In Northampton on August 29 a mob succeeded in keeping the courts closed to prevent debtors from being tried and imprisoned. Fearful of being tried for treason for this action, Shays and his followers broke up the state Supreme Court session at Springfield in September. The revolt escalated when Shays and a force of 1,200 men returned to Springfield in January to capture the arsenal. The national government fought back and prevented the attack on January 25. Most of the insurgents were captured by early February, ending the rebellion. The leaders were condemned to death for treason but were later pardoned. Shays himself later received a war pension for his service in the American Revolution.

Shays's Rebellion was one of several disturbances in different states. It hastened the movement for a federal government strong enough "to ensure domestic tranquility," as stated in the preamble to the U.S. Constitution.

to restrain the states from trade wars among themselves. And there was neither an executive to carry out the acts of Congress nor a federal court to interpret and enforce the laws.

CHAPTER TWO

A STRONGER, UNITED REPUBLIC

The Articles of Confederation sustained the Union through a critical period. However, the events of the years 1781 to 1787, including the national government's inability to act during Shays's Rebellion, showed that the Articles were unworkable. They deprived the national government of many essential powers, including direct taxation and the ability to regulate commerce between the states. George Washington, Alexander Hamilton, John Jay, James Madison, and other leaders repeatedly declared that the government ought to be strengthened. In the mid-1780s they began to do that.

TOWARD A NEW CONSTITUTION

The convention that wrote the United States Constitution was prepared for by a number of small steps. The first was a meeting in 1785 between representatives of Virginia and Maryland, called the Alexandria Conference, to

THE NEW NATION

Alexander Hamilton, shown here in a portrait painted by John Trumbull, was one of the Founding Fathers of the United States. He was the leading champion of a strong central government for the new nation.

settle disputes over the navigation of the Potomac River. Washington and Madison took the lead in having this meeting called. It proved so successful that Maryland went a step further and proposed that Pennsylvania, Delaware, Maryland, and Virginia should all appoint commissioners to meet and adopt a uniform commercial system. The shrewd Madison saw the opportunity of doing something still more important. He proposed a convention not of four states, but of all the states, to discuss the commercial conditions of the time and to devise an amendment to the Articles of Confederation. This convention was to meet in Annapolis, Maryland, in 1786.

When the time came, only five states sent representatives to the convention in Annapolis, and their opinions were far from harmonious. But Madison and Hamilton were both present and looking toward the future. They persuaded the representatives before adjourning to issue a call for a general convention of all the states to meet in Philadelphia, Pennsylvania, in May 1787. This was to be the Constitutional Convention. But because many people were suspicious of any such action, the call had to be made cautiously. It proposed that the gathering should "take into consideration the situation of the United States," and devise improvements in the government. Congress, after some hesitation, finally endorsed the plan, declaring that the states should send delegates for the sole and express purpose of revising the Articles of Confederation.

The plan for the convention had the warm support of Washington, Benjamin Franklin, and other eminent men. Virginia was the first state to choose delegates,

THE NEW NATION

Philadelphia's Independence Hall, shown here in a recent photo, was where both the Declaration of Independence and the U.S. Constitution were written and signed.

and it contributed greatly to the success of the undertaking by selecting Washington. Before the date set, 11 states had named their delegates. New Hampshire did not send its members until the work was well begun. Rhode Island refused to send any at all. The legislatures, not the people, chose the delegates.

A NOTABLE ASSEMBLY

The convention opened in Philadelphia on May 25. Among the 55 delegates were George Washington and James Madison (Virginia), Benjamin Franklin (Pennsylvania), and Alexander Hamilton (New York). Many of the delegates were lawyers, and most had government experience. Nearly all were wealthy.

Three principal rules were adopted. Each state would have one vote for any decisions the convention made.

Seven states of the 12 represented would constitute a quorum (the minimum number required to conduct business). The delegates were sworn to secrecy to avoid outside pressures.

A main issue was whether to merely revise the Articles or write a new constitution. Washington advised everyone to think long term. Within a week the convention resolved that "a national government ought to be established consisting of a supreme legislative, executive, and judiciary," and such leaders as Madison and Hamilton assumed that this meant a new constitution.

TIME FOR COMPROMISE

The convention faced two problems that loomed above all others. First, how would a stronger federal government wield authority? Would it be permitted to coerce the states? If so, how? In the second place, how was power to be divided fairly between the large (that is, more populous) states, such as Pennsylvania, and the small (less populous) states, such as Delaware? The Constitution in its final form was a bundle of compromises, but the great compromise was that between the large and small states.

Two important plans for creating a representative legislature came before the convention. The Virginia Plan, mostly pushed by James Madison, represented the standpoint of the large states and involved writing an entirely new constitution. It proposed a national legislature, or Congress, consisting of two chambers, or houses. The states were to be represented in Congress in proportion to their populations. Members of the lower house would be elected by the free citizens of a state. These elected members would choose the members of the upper house from lists submitted by the state legislatures. There would be a chief executive elected by Congress for a single term as well as a court system headed by a Supreme Court.

The New Jersey Plan represented the interests of the small states and was simply a set of amendments to the Articles of Confederation. It provided for a national congress of one house, in which each state would have a single vote. Congress would choose a chief executive, and there was to be a federal court system.

James Madison is known as the Father of the Constitution because of his key role in drafting the U.S. Constitution. As a member of Congress, he sponsored the Bill of Rights. Later he became the fourth president of the United States.

After heated debate on how to reconcile these plans, Connecticut delegates Roger Sherman and Oliver Ellsworth brought forward a successful compromise, called the Connecticut, or Great, Compromise. They proposed that the states be equally represented in the upper chamber, or Senate, and represented according to population in the lower chamber, or House of Representatives. After much grumbling the large states accepted this plan.

Another compromise dealt with federal regulation of commerce. The Northern states favored tighter regulations, while the Southern states feared export taxes on their cash crops, tobacco and cotton. The result was that

SLAVERY AND THE THREE-FIFTHS COMPROMISE

One of the compromises of the Constitutional Convention concerned how to count slaves for purposes of representation in Congress. The Southern states naturally demanded that they should be counted, while the Northern states wished them passed over as mere property. The Continental Congress had already provided a method of settling this dispute. In 1783, in a proposed amendment to the Articles of Confederation, it had decided that five slaves should count for three free persons when determining population. The delegates to the Constitutional Convention borrowed this idea, deciding that in determining representation in the House of Representatives, three-fifths of a state's slaves should be counted. This measure is known as the Three-Fifths Compromise.

Still another compromise had to do with the importation of slaves from Africa. Some Northerners would gladly have seen the slave trade abolished. Moreover, Virginia and Maryland "bred" slaves for the market and wished to stop the African competition. When Georgia and the Carolinas protested, a compromise provided that Congress might stop the importation in 1808 but not sooner.

This 19th-century engraving depicts slaves working on a Southern plantation. The delegates to the Constitutional Convention failed to end the cruel practice of slavery.

Congress was given wide powers over navigation, foreign and interstate trade, and custom duties, but it was specifically forbidden to levy export duties.

A STRONGER GOVERNMENT

As the summer wore on, the convention engineered a strong central government with now familiar features: the representatives chosen for two years and the senators for six; the president serving four years, with possible reelection; and the federal judges appointed for life.

One striking feature of the new Constitution was the large power given to Congress over economic and financial affairs. Not only was Congress authorized to regulate commerce, but it was given the right to raise money by taxation, to borrow on the national credit, and to coin money and regulate its value. Strict provisions were inserted forbidding the states to issue paper money or to pass laws impairing the obligation of contracts.

The great problem of how to give the federal government proper authority was finally solved with surprising ease. This was done by providing that the new government should operate not upon the states, but directly upon the people. Its mandates were to be carried out not by orders and demands upon a set of semi-independent state governments but by the quiet activity of its own administrative officers, attorneys, marshals, and courts. The two systems, state and federal, would for the most part operate on parallel lines. Whenever they did come into conflict, the Constitution would define their respective powers.

SEPARATION OF POWERS

To protect against abuses of power by the federal government, the makers of the Constitution provided for a "separation of powers." This means that the government is divided into three separate and independent bodies—the executive, legislative, and judicial branches. Through a system of "checks and balances," each branch of government is able to prevent actions by the other branches. In this way, the branches of government are made to share power, and no one branch gets too powerful. For example, the president (the head of the executive branch) can veto, or override, laws introduced and passed by Congress (the legislative branch). Congress can then override the president's veto if at least two-thirds of the members of each house vote to do so.

The separation of powers as well as checks and balances were designed to prevent tyranny and to secure the people's liberties—and thus to uphold the principles of the Declaration of Independence. John Adams stated: "It is by balancing each of these powers against the other two, that the efforts in human nature toward tyranny can alone be checked and restrained, and any degree of freedom preserved in the constitution."

THE LAW OF THE LAND

On September 17, 1787, 39 of the delegates signed a draft of the U.S. Constitution. It now had to be ratified, or approved, by nine of the 13 states. Two sides faced off in the ratification battle. The Federalists, led by Alexander

Hamilton, favored it. This group also included George Washington, John Jay, and James Madison. The Anti-Federalists included such leaders as Patrick Henry and Samuel Adams, who advocated local control and feared that the Constitution would lead to an undue concentration of authority. Many people declared, and with reason, that the Constitution was faulty because it contained no guarantee of the simplest human rights—freedom of speech, of the press, of assemblage, and of worship.

One by one the states held conventions to debate the new document. When New Hampshire voted its approval on June 21, 1788, the minimum number of nine states was met and the Constitution was officially ratified. By March 4, 1789, it was the official law of the land.

One thing that eased the fears of Anti-Federalists and those on the fence was the later addition of important constitutional amendments. The first 10, collectively known as the Bill of Rights, were adopted in December 1791. These amendments guaranteed a variety of individual rights and put limits on government power. They provided for freedom of speech, of the press, and of worship; for the right of the states to establish militia; for the security of people in their homes against unreasonable search and seizure; and for trial by jury. Particularly important is the Tenth Amendment, declaring that powers not delegated to the United States or prohibited to the states should be reserved to the states or to the people.

CHAPTER THREE

NEW CHALLENGES: THE REPUBLIC ENTERS THE 19ᵀᴴ CENTURY

The Constitution provided a solid foundation for the United States as it entered its first years of nationhood. Shifts in its political landscape, military conflict, geographic and industrial expansion, and social upheavals would mark the early decades of U.S. history. The country's economy, culture, and identity would begin to take shape during this turbulent but exciting era.

POLITICAL DEVELOPMENTS

The 11 states that had ratified the Constitution chose presidential electors early in 1789. All 69 electors voted for George Washington for president. John Adams was named vice president, and they were inaugurated on

THE NEW NATION

April 30. Meanwhile the House of Representatives and the Senate held their first sessions.

Washington did much to strengthen the central government. He was aided by Alexander Hamilton, his secretary of the treasury. Hamilton launched a series of measures to put the country on sound economic footing, including the creation of a national bank, the Bank of the United States. In foreign affairs Washington worked with Secretary of State Thomas Jefferson. They set up a policy of neutrality and fairness in dealing with other countries.

Disagreements over Hamilton's programs and over issues of foreign policy led to the emergence of national political parties. Jefferson, a strong supporter of states' rights, objected to Hamilton's efforts to strengthen the federal government. He joined with James Madison, now a congressman, to create the Democratic-Republican Party (later called the Democratic Party). This organization challenged Hamilton and his followers,

This portrait, *George Washington at Princeton*, was painted by Charles Peale Polk and was based on an earlier portrait by Polk's uncle, Charles Wilson Peale. Both honor Washington's 1777 victory in the Battle of Princeton during the American Revolution.

NEW CHALLENGES: THE REPUBLIC ENTERS THE 19TH CENTURY

The Bank of the United States was established in Philadelphia in 1791. Alexander Hamilton urged Congress to set up the bank to control the country's money supply and provide a convenient means of exchange for all the people of the United States.

who had formed the Federalist Party. In foreign affairs the Federalists favored ties with Britain, while the Democratic-Republicans backed France.

The young republic expanded its borders. In 1791 Vermont became the first state added to the original 13. Across the Appalachian Mountains, Kentucky became the first "western" state admitted to the Union, in 1792. Tennessee also gained statehood during George Washington's presidency, in 1796.

At the end of his second term as president, Washington refused to run for a third. His successor was John Adams, his vice president. Adams was an able president, but he lacked Washington's popularity. In anticipation of war with France, Adams's Federalist Party enacted the very controversial Alien and Sedition Acts. They imposed serious civil restrictions on aliens suspected of pro-French activities and penalized U.S. citizens who criticized the government.

THE JEFFERSONIAN ERA

Adams sought reelection in 1800 but was defeated by Thomas Jefferson, the Democratic-Republican candidate. Jefferson's inauguration in 1801 began 28 consecutive years of Democratic-Republican rule. Reelected in 1804, Jefferson is remembered as a chief architect of American democracy. He also did much to push the nation's western frontier. In 1803 he ordered Meriwether Lewis and William Clark to make an overland journey to the Pacific Ocean. That same year he made the famous

The author of the Declaration of Independence in 1776, Thomas Jefferson was later the third president of the United States, serving from 1801 to 1809.

THE LOUISIANA PURCHASE

The United States, like other nations, wanted to expand its control to its "natural boundaries." America's western settlers, especially farmers eager to move their products, wanted the port of New Orleans and the Mississippi River to be under U.S. control.

When Spain was forced to give up New Orleans to France in 1802, Americans were worried. But the United States would soon benefit from the overseas conflict between Britain and France. Britain defeated France's navy and thus controlled the seas. Without access to its vast North American territory, France decided to sell it to the United States.

President Jefferson sent James Monroe to France as an envoy to negotiate the purchase of New Orleans. He was shocked when Napoleon offered to sell the whole Louisiana Territory for $15,000,000. It was an incredible bargain for 828,000 square miles (2,145,000 square kilometers) of land. Thus at one stroke the area of the United States was doubled.

Out of this territory would be carved the entire states of Missouri, Arkansas, Iowa, North Dakota, South Dakota, Nebraska, and Oklahoma, as well as Louisiana. In addition, the Louisiana Purchase included most of what are now the states of Kansas, Colorado, Wyoming, Montana, and Minnesota.

THE NEW NATION

Louisiana Purchase. Also in 1803, Ohio was admitted to the Union, the first of five states formed from the Northwest Territory.

This map depicts the United States in 1803, the year of the Louisiana Purchase. The acquisition of Louisiana from France added 828,000 square miles (2,145,00 square kilometers) of territory to the United States, doubling the country's size.

During Jefferson's tenure two other events helped guide the nation's course. In 1803 in the case of *Marbury v. Madison*, the Supreme Court declared an act of Congress unconstitutional. This established the important principle of judicial review of legislation. The second event was congressional action halting the importation of slaves into the United States after 1807.

Foreign affairs caused the United States much concern in the early 1800s. Pirates from the Barbary States of North Africa attacked American trading ships. They were finally defeated by U.S. forces in the war against Tripoli in 1801–05. War between Britain and France also interfered with American shipping.

WAR AND PEACE

James Madison, an ally of Jefferson's, handily won the presidential election of 1808. As Jefferson's secretary of state, he had criticized Britain and France for preying on U.S. ships. Britain had further provoked Americans with its policy of impressment, by which U.S. sailors were seized and forced into service in the British navy.

Tensions with Britain grew during Madison's presidency. Encouraged by the so-called War Hawks in Congress, Madison signed a declaration of war on June 18, 1812. Thus began the War of 1812. The American leaders expected to conquer British-controlled Canada in short order, but the government was totally unprepared for war. The regular army was poorly drilled and officered, and New England strongly opposed the war. These conditions brought quick disaster to the early U.S. campaign to take Canada. Despite these setbacks, Madison was reelected in 1812.

In August 1814 the British marched into Washington, D.C., and burned parts of the city, including the Capitol and the president's home. After capturing Alexandria, Virginia, the British were stopped in September by U.S. forces at Fort McHenry in Baltimore, Maryland. This battle was made famous when Francis Scott Key wrote about it in a poem that eventually

NEW CHALLENGES: THE REPUBLIC ENTERS THE 19TH CENTURY

provided the lyrics to the U.S. national anthem, "The Star-Spangled Banner."

This illustration depicts British forces burning government buildings in Washington, D.C., in 1814, during the War of 1812. This attack was the only time in U.S. history that foreign troops occupied the capital.

By this time both sides were tired of the war. Peace discussions began at Ghent in Belgium in August 1814, and a treaty was signed on December 24. However, news of the peace did not come in time to prevent a bloody battle at New Orleans, Louisiana. There U.S. General Andrew Jackson quickly and decisively beat back a British invasion on January 8, 1815, two weeks after peace was declared. Jackson's reputation as a war hero would later help his political fortunes.

Though neither side had won a clear victory in the war, the United States had survived and proven itself on the world stage. Many Americans proclaimed the result a U.S. triumph. Meanwhile, the Federalists'

NEW CHALLENGES: THE REPUBLIC ENTERS THE 19TH CENTURY

In the Battle of New Orleans, U.S. forces led by General Andrew Jackson defeated British forces that attacked New Orleans on January 8, 1815. Word had not reached the combatants that a treaty had already ended the War of 1812 two weeks earlier.

bitter opposition to the war and divisions within the party helped to seal the party's downfall. In 1816 another Democratic-Republican, James Monroe, was elected to the presidency.

"THE ERA OF GOOD FEELING"

With the political demise of the Federalists, Monroe's two-term presidency (1817–25) was seen as a time of growing national unity. It is sometimes called the "Era of Good Feeling" because of the lack of partisan rivalry. Monroe's presidency brought growing national wealth, westward expansion, and infrastructure development.

Monroe, who had helped negotiate the Louisiana Purchase as Jefferson's ambassador, is also famous for the Monroe Doctrine. This hugely influential foreign-policy statement declared that the United States would not interfere in European affairs and, in turn, that the United States would not permit any European nation to extend its holdings or use armed force on the two American continents. Any violation would be considered a hostile act against the United States.

At the beginning of Monroe's presidency U.S. authorities were attempting to recapture runaway slaves who had fled to Spanish-held Florida to live among the Seminole people. The escaped slaves had joined the Seminole in raiding U.S. settlements in Georgia. When Spain refused to intervene in this matter, Monroe sent General Andrew Jackson to suppress these raids. Jackson led a U.S. invasion into Florida in what became known as the First Seminole War. As a result of the war, Spain ceded Florida to the United States in 1819. Monroe also faced the country's first conflict over slavery, which was settled only temporarily by the Missouri Compromise of 1820.

During the presidential election of 1824, the "good feeling" was replaced with a heated four-way race between Henry Clay, John Quincy Adams, William H. Crawford, and Andrew Jackson. Though Jackson won the popular vote, none of the candidates received a majority of the electoral votes. Thus the election fell to the House of Representatives. Adams, former president John Adams's eldest son, was named president, much to the disgust of Jackson and his followers. Largely because of relentless opposition from Jackson's supporters, John Quincy Adams was an unsuccessful president.

JACKSONIAN DEMOCRACY

In the election of 1828, Adams's National Republican Party faced off against Andrew Jackson and his Democratic Party (a new version of the Democratic-Republican Party). Jackson was elected, becoming the first president from the new West. He was also a symbol of the political power of the common people.

Jackson asserted the supremacy of the national government during a crisis over Southern opposition to a tariff

THE NEW NATION

This 1841 print by Robert Cruikshank, entitled *President's Levee, or All Creation Going to the White House*, shows a crowd gathered in front of the White House for the inauguration of Andrew Jackson in 1829.

NEW CHALLENGES: THE REPUBLIC ENTERS THE 19TH CENTURY

on industrial goods. The Southern states felt that the tariff favored the North at the expense of the South. Jackson's vice president, John C. Calhoun of South Carolina, argued that states could nullify, or declare invalid, federal laws within their boundaries. Jackson, however, vowed to use military force to collect the tariff. The so-called nullification crisis ended with a compromise tariff in 1833.

A long-standing conflict over the Bank of the United States came to a head during Jackson's presidency. Jackson led the opposition to the national bank, calling it an enemy of democracy and the common people. His political rivals, led by Henry Clay, made the fate of the bank the central issue of the 1832 presidential election.

THE NEW NATION

Andrew Jackson was the first U.S. president to gain office by a direct appeal to the mass of voters. His political movement championing popular democracy and the common man has become known as Jacksonian Democracy.

Jackson decisively defeated Clay to win reelection and worked to dismantle the bank during his second term. The bank would eventually go out of business in 1841, ending the so-called Bank War.

CHAPTER FOUR

THE COMPLICATED LEGACY OF WESTERN EXPANSION

The United States grew dramatically in its early decades. Industry and trade grew in the North, while plantation agriculture expanded in the South. At the same time, the westward expansion of the United States seemed unstoppable.

This growth was complicated, however. Westward expansion brought American settlers in conflict with the Native Americans who already occupied the land. The lengthy and brutal conflict between Indians and whites would become one of the most tragic chapters in the country's history.

Westward expansion also focused attention on the increasingly divisive issue of slavery. Plantation agriculture had made the South one of the world's most important agricultural producers. This success would not have been possible without the labor of slaves. The question of whether slavery should be extended into newly settled territories would lead to conflict throughout the expansion era.

SETTLING THE FRONTIER

The government of the United States had hardly been launched when a major battle between Indians and settlers in the Northwest Territory erupted in 1789. Peace was not restored until 1794, when General Anthony Wayne crushed the Indians' power in the Battle of Fallen Timbers near Maumee, Ohio. In the resulting Treaty of Greenville, the Indians ceded to the United States most of Ohio and parts of Indiana, Illinois, and Michigan. The treaty gave a great impetus to westward migration and settlement of this area, the first "West."

As settlers intruded further on Indian lands, the Shawnee leader Tecumseh organized a confederation of tribes to resist further settlement. The Indians were soon routed, however, by armies led by two future presidents. In 1811 General William Henry Harrison beat a group of Shawnee led by Tecumseh's brother Tenskwatawa in the Battle of Tippecanoe (Indiana). In the South, General Andrew Jackson crushed the Creek tribe in the Battle of Horseshoe Bend (Alabama) in 1814. After that, there was no major Indian resistance east of the Mississippi.

THE COMPLICATED LEGACY OF WESTERN EXPANSION

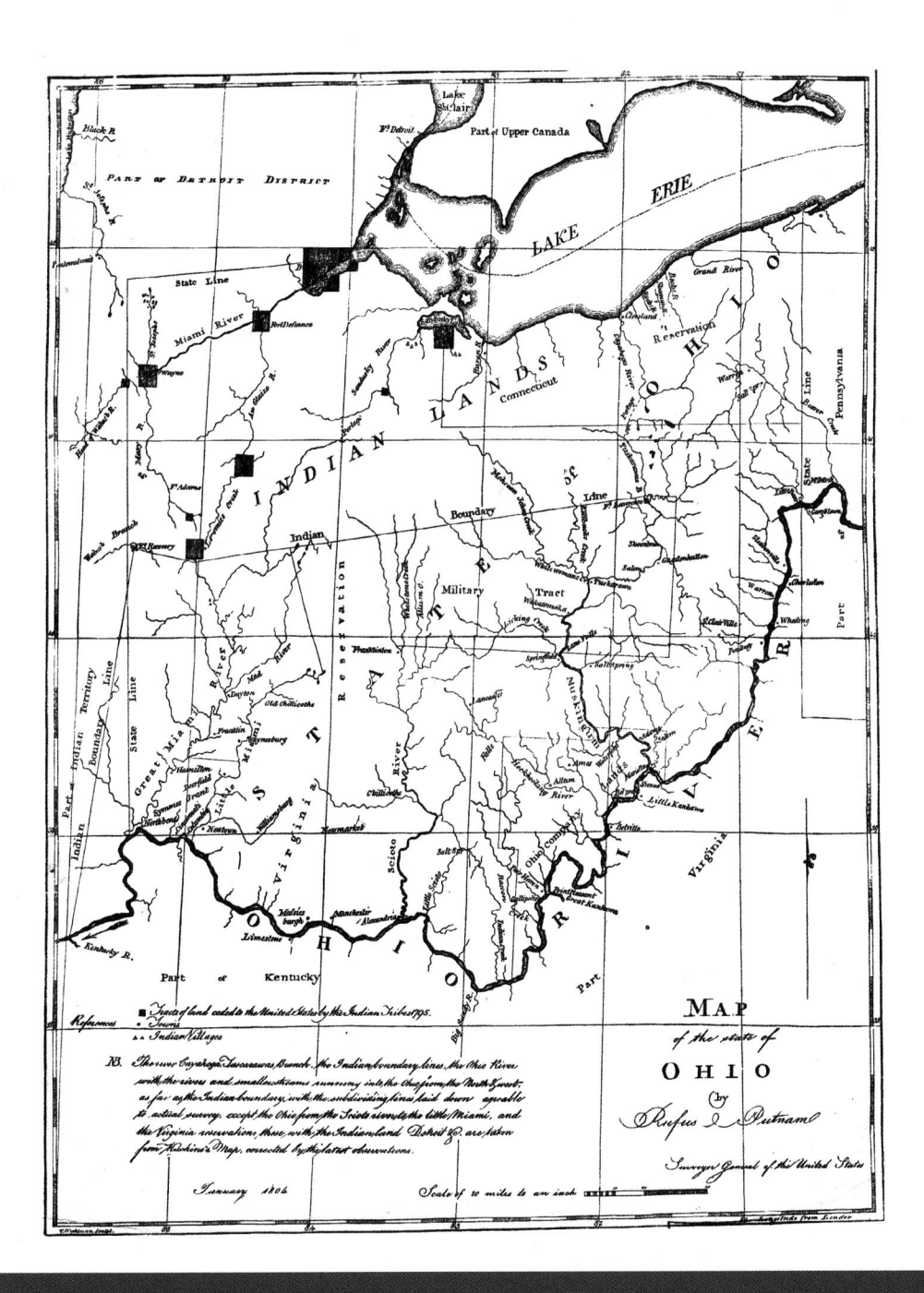

This 1804 map of Ohio underscores the continuing presence of Native Americans on land the United States had claimed. Ohio was the first state carved out of the Northwest Territory and one of the battlegrounds of the Indian wars the new nation waged.

After the War of 1812 there was a steady rush of immigration into what is now the Midwest. Small farmers populated the lake plains in the North. Cotton planters founded plantations in the Gulf plains in the South. The Mississippi Valley attracted both kinds of farmers. By 1850 the eastern half of the American continent was well settled. Thousands more had poured across the Mississippi River into Iowa, Missouri, Arkansas, and Louisiana.

THE "INDIAN PROBLEM"

During the westward expansion, settlers and the U.S. government treated the American Indians as an obstacle. The government's method of dealing with the "Indian problem" evolved over the years. Beginning in the 1770s the government negotiated treaties with certain Indian tribes. Typically the tribes agreed to turn over much of their land to the United States in exchange for money, goods, and promises that U.S. citizens would not settle in the tribes' remaining territory. These treaties were considered to be agreements between two sovereign nations. Nevertheless, the terms were routinely violated as settlers continued to trespass on Indian lands.

After the War of 1812 the federal government no longer treated the Indians as peoples of separate nations. Rather, they were considered wards of the United States, to be relocated at the convenience of the government. In 1830 this policy was made law when President Andrew Jackson signed the Indian Removal Act. The act authorized the president to remove tribes

Osceola led the Seminole people in resisting U.S. encroachment in Florida in the Second Seminole War (1835–42). Captured by U.S. troops in 1837, he died while imprisoned in 1838.

THE TRAIL OF TEARS

The Cherokee, a Southeast Indian tribe, resisted removal from their eastern homeland by turning to the U.S. courts. In 1832 the U.S. Supreme Court ruled in favor of the tribe in the landmark case *Worcester v. Georgia*. Georgia ignored the decision, however, with Jackson's backing. The federal government aggressively followed a policy of resettlement in the Indian Territory (later Oklahoma) beyond the Mississippi. In one of American history's most shameful moments, the Cherokee, along with the rest of the eastern Indian tribes—including the Chickasaw, Creek, Choctaw, and Seminole peoples—were driven westward along the Trail of Tears. During the 1830s some 100,000 Indians were forced from their homes and relocated. About 15,000 died of illness and malnutrition during the grueling trip.

from their land east of the Mississippi and resettle them west of the river.

SLAVERY: A LEGACY OF CRUELTY

Just as the Northeast and West were growing in population and developing their unique economies and

The cotton gin, invented by Eli Whitney in 1793, made cotton growing with slave labor highly profitable in the South and thus played a large role in expanding plantation agriculture.

regional cultures, so was the South. The great majority of Southerners were tied in some way to agriculture, and much of this activity depended on the large population of African and African-descended slaves who worked the land.

During the 17th and 18th centuries African slaves harvested tobacco, rice, and indigo on the Southern seaboard. In 1793 Eli Whitney, a Northern inventor, created the cotton gin. The device, which removed seeds from cotton, increased cotton production more than twentyfold by 1800 and also greatly expanded the crop into the Deep South. The growth in cotton production increased the demand for slaves. Sugar was another major Southern crop worked by slaves.

THE LIVES OF SLAVES

The huge cotton and sugar plantations brought prosperity to the South but great hardship to the slaves. Slaves experienced harsh work conditions and punishment and were often completely at the mercy of their owners. Whippings and beatings were common, as was the forced separation of families when slaves were sold off to others. Slaves had few or no protections or rights under the law.

The official end of the African slave trade in 1808 spurred the growth of the domestic slave trade in the United States, especially as a source of labor for the new cotton lands in the Southern interior. Increasingly, the supply of slave came to be supplemented by the practice of "slave breeding," in which women slaves were encouraged—and often forced—to conceive as early as 13 years of age and to give birth as often as possible.

Laws known as slave codes ensured absolute control by the master and complete submission by the slave. Under these laws the slave was a chattel—a piece of property and a source of labor that could be bought and sold like an animal. Slaves were allowed no stable family life and little privacy. They

THE COMPLICATED LEGACY OF WESTERN EXPANSION

were prohibited by law from learning to read or write. The meek slave received tokens of favor from the master; the rebellious slave provoked brutal punishment. A social hierarchy among plantation slaves kept them divided. At the

Black slaves played a major, though unwilling and unrewarded, role in America's economic foundation—especially in the South. Blacks also had great influence on Southern culture, including speech, folklore, music, dancing, and food.

top were the house slaves; next were the skilled artisans; and at the bottom were the vast majority of field hands, who bore the brunt of harsh plantation life.

RESISTANCE AND REVOLT

Because of this tight control, there were few successful slave revolts. Slave plots were invariably betrayed. Some slave revolts, such as those of Gabriel Prosser (Richmond, Virginia, in 1800) and Denmark Vesey (Charleston, South Carolina, in 1822), were elaborately planned. The slave revolt that was perhaps most frightening to whites was the one led by Nat Turner, in Southampton, Virginia, in 1831. Before Turner and his coconspirators were captured, they had killed about sixty whites.

Individual slaves also found ways to protest their condition. This resistance took such forms as mothers killing their newborn children to save them from slavery, the poisoning of slave owners, destruction of machinery and crops, arson, malingering, and running away.

THE POLITICS OF SLAVERY

The extension of slavery to new territories had been a national political controversy since the Northwest Ordinance of 1787 prohibited slavery in the area now known as the Midwest. The states of the North abolished slavery between 1777 and 1804, but slavery remained legal and very profitable in the South. The

North and the South grew more and more different, in both economy and social attitudes.

Tensions over slavery had been kept in check by maintaining a balance between slave states, in which slavery was allowed, and free states, in which it was outlawed. By 1819 the United States had 22 states, evenly divided between slave and free states. This balance was threatened when Missouri asked to be admitted to the Union as a slave state. The resulting political debate brought the slavery issue to the public's attention in a dramatic way. In 1820 Congress passed a compromise that permitted Missouri to enter as a slave state and Maine as a free state. The Missouri Compromise defused tensions for a while, but the struggle would ignite again in the coming decades.

CHAPTER FIVE

A NEW AND CHANGING AMERICA

During the 1970s more than 90 percent of Americans lived on farms. There were already definite signs, however, that the country would develop an industrial economy. Industrialization would have a profound effect not only on the nation's economy but also on its settlement patterns, as the population would gradually become more urban. Advances in transportation opened up more of the country for the movement of people and goods. Social developments helped to shape a still- evolving American identity.

THE EARLY INDUSTRIAL REVOLUTION

The change from an agricultural, handicraft economy to one dominated by industry and machine manufacture is known as the Industrial Revolution. The Industrial Revolution began in Britain in the 18th century and from there spread to other parts of the world.

The United States was slow in adopting machine methods of manufacture. Farming and trading would remain its chief interests until the 1860s. The new nation had little capital with which to buy the machinery and put up the buildings required. Such capital as existed was largely invested in shipping and commerce. Labor was scarce because Americans continued to push westward, clearing the forests and establishing themselves on the land.

A start in manufacturing, however, was made in New England in 1793 by Samuel Slater. A skilled textile worker, he immigrated to the United States from England and opened the country's first successful cotton mill in Pawtucket, Rhode Island. When the Napoleonic Wars in Europe and the War of 1812 upset commerce and made English products difficult to obtain, more American investors began to build factories.

New England soon developed an important textile industry. It had swift streams for power and a humid climate, which kept cotton and wool fibers in condition for spinning and weaving. In Pennsylvania iron for machines, tools, and guns was smelted in stone furnaces. They burned charcoal, plentiful in this forested land. Spinning machines driven by steam were operating in New York by 1810. The first practical power loom was installed at Waltham, Massachusetts, by Francis Cabot Lowell in 1814. Shoemaking was organized into

Built in 1793, Slater Mill was the first successful cotton mill in the United States. The water-powered mill was located on the banks of the Blackstone River in Pawtucket, Rhode Island. Founded by Samuel Slater, it started the American cotton textile industry.

early 19th century. New England was the first area in the United States to industrialize.

Techniques of factory production were refined in American workshops. Eli Whitney led the movement to standardize parts used in manufacture. They became interchangeable, enabling unskilled workers to assemble products from boxes of parts quickly. American factories used machine tools to make parts. These machines were arranged in lines for more efficient production. This was called the "American system of manufacturing," and it was admired by all other industrial nations. It was first applied to the manufacture of firearms and later spread to other industries like clock and lock making.

The country's economic expansion would not have been possible without a great supply of capital—money, machinery, and other resources that are used to produce goods and services. The need to raise large sums of capital led to the development of corporations. At the same time, the economy became increasingly specialized through a division of labor. As people focused their efforts in certain types of work, production became more efficient and the number, variety, and quality of goods all increased. Such developments signaled the rise of capitalism in the United States.

The growth of the American economy was encouraged by great advances in transportation. In 1807 Robert Fulton launched the first successful steamboat, the *Clermont*, in the Hudson River. Five years later the

THE NEW NATION

New Orleans became the first steamboat to navigate the Mississippi River. Meanwhile, in 1811, the Cumberland Road (National Pike) was started westward from Cumberland, Maryland. Also important was the Erie Canal, which was completed in 1825. This great waterway linked the Hudson River with the Great Lakes. Soon canal development would be overtaken by the growth of the railroads, which covered great distances much more efficiently. Work on the Baltimore and Ohio line, the first railroad in the United States, began in 1828.

A NEW AND CHANGING AMERICA 63

This painting by Anthony Imbert, entitled *Erie Canal Celebration*, dates from 1825, the year of the canal's completion. The canal's success propelled New York City into a major commercial center and encouraged canal construction throughout the country.

FREE BLACKS DURING THE SLAVE ERA

During the slavery era, free blacks made up about one-tenth of the country's black population. The earliest African American leaders emerged among the free blacks of the North, particularly those of Philadelphia, Pennsylvania; Boston, Massachusetts; and New York City. These free blacks established their own institutions—churches, schools, and mutual aid societies. One of the first of these organizations was the African Methodist Episcopal (AME) Church, formed in 1816 and led by Bishop Richard Allen of Philadelphia. Among other noted free blacks was the astronomer and mathematician Benjamin Banneker.

Free blacks were among the first abolitionists. They included John B. Russwurm and Samuel E. Cornish, who in 1827 founded *Freedom's Journal*, the first African American–run newspaper in the United States. Black support also permitted the founding and survival of the *Liberator*, a journal begun in 1831 by the white abolitionist William Lloyd Garrison. Probably the most-celebrated of all African American journals was the *North Star*, founded in 1847 by the former slave Frederick Douglass, who argued that the antislavery movement must be led by black people.

Beginning in 1830 African American leaders met regularly in national and state conventions. But they differed on the best strategies to use against slavery and discrimination. Some, such as David Walker and Henry Highland Garnet, called on slaves to revolt. Others, such as Russwurm and Paul Cuffe, proposed that a major modern black country be established in Africa. Supported by the American Colonization Society, whose membership was overwhelmingly white, African Americans founded Liberia in West Africa in 1822.

Bethel African Methodist Episcopal Church was established by Richard Allen in Philadelphia in 1794. In 1816 it was joined by other eastern black congregations to form the African Methodist Episcopal Church, the first independent black denomination in the United States..

SOCIAL DEVELOPMENTS

The economic growth of the early 1800s brought social changes to the United States. Many people moved from rural areas to work in the new factories. The mass of industrial laborers formed a new working class, while the factory owners belonged to the middle class. Factory workers tended to cluster together in the cities, forming working-class neighborhoods with typically poor living conditions. In the early decades of industrialization the U.S. workforce included many young unmarried women, especially in the textile mills. Child labor was also common. The textile mill opened in Pawtucket in 1790 employed nine children between the ages of seven and 12.

As slavery declined in the North following the American Revolution, newly freed slaves began to establish communities of their own. For a few years free blacks enjoyed considerable freedom of movement. But in the 1790s and after, the status of free blacks deteriorated as states adopted laws restricting their activities, residences, and economic choices. In general they came to occupy poor neighborhoods and grew into a permanent underclass, denied education and opportunity.

The American Revolution had also shown the economic importance of women. Women had always contributed greatly to the operation of farms and often businesses, but they rarely achieved independent status. While the men were off fighting the war, however, women proved that they were capable of taking full charge. After the war, women began talking more about their rights, education, and role in society. Some states changed their laws to allow women to inherit a share of estates and to have limited control of property after marriage. On the whole, however, the American Revolution itself had only very gradual and limited effects on women's status. The changes that took place stopped far short of making women into independent citizens of equal political and civil status with men.

RELIGIOUS LIFE

Religion continued to be an important influence on American life in the early years of the United States, as it had been during the colonial era. A religious revival movement known as the Second Great Awakening began in New England in the 1790s and quickly spread nationwide, lasting until the 1830s. The original Great Awakening, which had swept the colonies from the 1720s to the 1740s, was a fiery evangelical movement that arose in response to the increasing secularization of society.

The Second Great Awakening, though less emotional than the original, nevertheless inspired renewed missionary and educational efforts and produced a large increase in church membership. It led to the founding of many colleges and seminaries and to the organization of mission societies. It also created support for a variety of moral and social reform movements, including for temperance, the abolition of slavery, and women's rights. These movements would have profound effects on American society in the years to come.

CONCLUSION

In the decades following the American Revolution, the United States established itself as one of the world's great democracies. This was due largely to the efforts of the Founding Fathers. After leading the war for independence from Great Britain, these statesmen made far-reaching decisions that laid the foundation for the new nation.

The Founders created the first modern country based on liberal principles. These include the democratic principle that political power should belong to the citizens, rather than to a king or queen. The Founders emphasized the importance of the rights of the individual, rather than society or the government. Finally, they built the United States as a capitalist country, with the principle that economic productivity depends on individual initiative in the marketplace rather than on state-sponsored policies. This liberal formula was later adopted by countries throughout the world, replacing European monarchies in the 19th century and the totalitarian regimes of Germany, Japan, and the Soviet Union in the 20th century.

Despite these great achievements, the Founders also had two crucial failures. One was their inability to end slavery. Slavery was incompatible with the values of the American Revolution, and all the prominent members of the Revolutionary generation acknowledged that fact. The Founders ended the slave trade in 1808 and made slavery illegal in the North. However, they failed to act in the South. They eventually insisted that the legality of slavery was a matter for the individual states to decide, not the national government. Ultimately, slavery became so entrenched that it took a war—the American Civil War—to end it.

The other tragic failure of the Founders was the inability to implement a just policy toward the Native Americans. As the new nation pushed relentlessly westward onto Indian lands, a question arose: How could the legitimate rights of the Indians be reconciled with those of the growing population of white settlers?

In the end, they could not. The United States forced the Indians off their land and relocated them to reservations in the West. Although the government's policy of Indian removal was not officially implemented until 1830, the seeds of the policy were planted during the founding era. The nation's westward expansion would continue to create conflict and suffering for the Indians throughout the 19th century.

TIMELINE

1781 The first national government of the United States is organized under the Articles of Confederation.

1786-87 Shays's Rebellion helps convince many Americans that the nation needs a stronger central governmental.

1787 The Constitutional Convention draws up the U.S. Constitution. Upon ratification in 1788, it replaces the Articles of Confederation as the law of the land.

1789 George Washington is elected the first president of the United States.

1796 John Adams is elected president.

1800 Thomas Jefferson is elected president.

1803 The Louisiana Purchase doubles the size of the United States.

1804-06 The Lewis and Clark Expedition explores the Louisiana Purchase and the Pacific Northwest.

1808 James Madison is elected president.

1811 Construction begins on the Cumberland Road (National Pike), the first highway built by the federal government.

1812 Louisiana is admitted to the Union.

1812 The War of 1812 breaks out.

1814 The Treaty of Ghent ends the War of 1812.

1816 Indiana is admitted to the Union.

1817 Mississippi is admitted to the Union.

1818 James Madison is elected president. Illinois is admitted to the Union.

1819 Alabama is admitted to the Union.

1820 Congress passes the Missouri Compromise, which allows Missouri to join the Union as a slave state and Maine to join as a free state.

1824 John Quincy Adams is elected president.

1825 The Erie Canal is completed, connecting the Great Lakes region to New York City via the Hudson River.

1828 Andrew Jackson is elected president. Work begins on the Baltimore and Ohio line, the nation's first railroad.

1830 Congress passes the Indian Removal Act, authorizing President Jackson to relocate all Native Americans living east of the Mississippi River to the West.

GLOSSARY

abolitionism The movement to abolish, or end, the institution of slavery and the Atlantic slave trade in the 18th and 19th centuries.

act A law made by a group of legislators.

Bill of Rights The first 10 amendments to the United States Constitution.

capitalism A way of organizing an economy so that the things that are used to make and transport products (such as land, oil, factories, ships, etc.) are owned by individual people and companies rather than by the government.

Congress The legislative branch of the U.S. federal government.

doctrine A statement of government policy, especially in international relations.

export A product that is sent to another country to be sold there.

House of Representatives The lower house of the U.S. Congress.

import A product brought into a country to be sold there.

neutrality The quality or state of not supporting either side in an argument, fight, or war.

nullification The constitutional theory that a state could nullify, or declare legally invalid, a federal act within the state's boundaries.

Senate The upper house of the U.S. Congress.

slavery The state of being a slave or the practice of owning slaves.

temperance movement Movement dedicated to promoting moderation and, more often, complete abstinence in the use of alcohol.

treaty An official agreement that is made between two or more countries or groups.

FOR MORE INFORMATION

American Historical Association
400 A Street SE
Washington, DC 20003
(202) 544-2422
Website: https://www.historians.org
The American Historical Association (AHA) is dedicated to the study and promotion of history and historical thinking.

Journal of American History
1215 E. Atwater Avenue
Bloomington, IN 47401-3703
(812) 855–2816
Website: http://www.journalofamericanhistory.org
The *Journal of American History* is a leading publication in the field of American history.

The Library of Congress
101 Independence Avenue SE
Washington, DC 20540
(202) 707-5000
Website: https://www.loc.gov
The Library of Congress is the largest library in the world, with millions of books, recordings, photographs, maps, and manuscripts in its collections. It is also the national library of the United States.

The National Archives and Records Administration
8601 Adelphi Road
College Park, MD 20740-6001
(866) 272-6272
Website: http://www.archives.gov
The National Archives and Records Administration (NARA) is dedicated to preserving valuable historical records and making them available to the public

Nineteenth Century Studies Association (NCSA)
University of Nebraska
6001 Dodge Street
Omaha, NE 68182
(402) 554-2598
Website: http://www.ncsaweb.net
The Nineteenth Century Studies Association promotes scholarship on political, social, economic, and artistic developments of the 19th century, both within the United States and worldwide.

Organization of American Historians (OAH)
112 N. Bryan Avenue
Bloomington, IN 47408-4141
(812) 855-7311
Website: http://www.oah.org
The Organization of American Historians (OAH) was founded in 1907 and is the largest professional society dedicated to the teaching and study of American history.

FOR MORE INFORMATION

Thomas Jefferson Foundation
P.O. Box 316
Charlottesville, VA 22902
(434) 984-9800
Website: http://www.monticello.org
The Thomas Jefferson Foundation owns and maintains more than half of Jefferson's 5,000-acre plantation, Monticello.

WEBSITES

Because of the changing nature of Internet links, Rosen Publishing has developed an online list of websites related to the subject of this book. This site is updated regularly. Please use this link to access the list:

http://www.rosenlinks.com/EAH/New

BIBLIOGRAPHY

Bilder, Mary Sarah. *Madison's Hand: Revising the Constitutional Convention*. Cambridge, MA: Harvard University Press, 2015.

Chernow, Ron. *Washington: A Life*. New York, NY: Penguin, 2011.

Künstler, Mort, and Edward G. Lengel. *The New Nation: The Creation of the United States in Paintings and Eyewitness Accounts*. New York, NY: Sterling, 2014.

McCullough, David G. *1776*. New York, NY: Simon & Schuster, 2006.

Meacham, Jon. *Thomas Jefferson: The Art of Power*. New York, NY: Random House, 2013.

Rakove, Jack N., and George Stade. *Founding America: Documents from the Revolution to the Bill of Rights*. New York, NY: Barnes & Noble Classics, 2006.

Stewart, David O. *The Summer of 1787: The Men Who Invented the Constitution*. New York, NY: Simon & Schuster, 2008.

INDEX

A

Adams, John, 29, 31, 34
Adams, John Quincy, 43
agriculture/farms, 14, 16, 47–48, 50, 52–53, 58
Alexandria Conference, 19–21
American Revolution, 6, 9, 14, 16, 66, 67, 69
Anti-Federalists, 30
Articles of Confederation, 6, 10–12, 13–14, 19, 21, 24, 25, 26

B

Bank of the United States, 32, 45–46

C

capitalism, 61, 69
Clay, Henry, 43, 45–46
commerce, 6, 15, 19, 26–28, 59
confederation of states, 6, 12, 13–18
Congress, 24–28, 29, 37, 38
Connecticut (Great) Compromise, 25–26
Constitution, U.S., 6, 19, 24, 28–30, 31
Constitutional Convention, 21–28
Continental Congress, 10, 12, 13, 16–18, 21, 26
Crawford, William H., 43

D

Declaration of Independence, 10, 29
Democratic-Republican Party, 32–33, 34, 42, 43

E

Era of Good Feeling, 42, 43

F

Federalist Party, 33, 34, 40–42
Federalists, 29–30
First Seminole War, 43
foreign affairs, 8, 14, 32, 33, 37, 42
Founding Fathers, 8, 69
France, 8, 33, 34, 37
Franklin, Benjamin, 21, 23

G

Great Britain, 6, 8, 9, 12, 15, 16, 33, 37–38

H

Hamilton, Alexander, 19, 21, 23, 29–30, 32
House of Representatives, 26, 28, 32, 43

I

industrial economy, 47, 58–62, 66
Industrial Revolution, 58–59

J

Jackson, Andrew, 40, 43–46, 48, 50, 52
Jay, John, 19, 30
Jefferson, Thomas, 32, 34–37, 42

L

Louisiana Purchase, 36, 42

M

Madison, James, 19, 21, 23, 24, 30, 32, 37–38
Mississippi River, 9, 15, 50, 52
Missouri Compromise, 43, 57
money, issuing of, 8, 16, 28
Monroe, James, 42
Monroe Doctrine, 42

N

Native Americans/Indians, 12, 42–43, 47, 48, 70
   Indian Removal Act, 50, 70
   Trail of Tears, 52
Northwest Ordinance, 14, 56

P

Paris, Treaty of, 9, 14
political developments, 31–34, 42

R

religious life, 67–68

S

Second Great Awakening, 67–68
Senate, 25, 28, 32
separation of powers, 29
Shays's Rebellion, 16–17, 19
Slater, Samuel, 59
slavery, 52–57
   abolitionists, 64–65, 68
   "breeding" of slaves, 26–27, 54
   conflicts over, 43, 47–48, 56–57, 70
   escaped slaves, 42–43
   free blacks during, 64–65, 66
   importation of slaves, 26–27, 37, 54, 69
   lives of slaves, 54–55
   politics of, 56, 69–70
   resistance and revolt, 56, 65
   Three-Fifths Compromise, 26–27
social developments, 58, 66–67
Spain, 9, 15–16, 42–43
Supreme Court, 25, 37, 52

T

taxation, 6, 12, 14, 16–18, 19, 26, 28, 43–45
transportation, 58, 61–62

W

War of 1812, 38–42, 48, 50, 59
Washington, George, 9, 19, 21, 23, 24, 30, 31–32, 33–34
western expansion, 34–36, 47–57, 59, 70
women, status of, 66–67, 68

DISCARDED BY MEMPHIS PUBLIC LIBRARY

Randolph

NOV 0 5 2009

The Disenfranchisement of African American Males

The Disenfranchisement of African American Males

Analysis of an American Tradition

Completed in association with:

The JAMAR Institute

"Bringing Communities Full Circle."
www.thejamarinstitute.com

Dr. Ron Davis

Copyright © 2008 by Dr. Ron Davis.

Library of Congress Control Number: 2008903548
ISBN: Hardcover   978-1-4363-3700-7
               Softcover   978-1-4363-3699-4

All rights reserved. No part of this book may be reproduced or transmitted in any form or by any means, electronic or mechanical, including photocopying, recording, or by any information storage and retrieval system, without permission in writing from the copyright owner.

This book was printed in the United States of America.

To order additional copies of this book, contact:
Xlibris Corporation
1-888-795-4274
www.Xlibris.com
Orders@Xlibris.com
48921

CONTENTS

Preface 9
Definition of Key Terms 13

1. Defining Disenfranchisement
   in the African American Community 15
2. Educational Disenfranchisement 22
3. Understanding the Policymaking Process
   to end Disenfranchisement 31
4. Economic Disenfranchisement 43
5. Sociopolitical Disenfranchisement 50
6. Research: Memphis, Tennessee 54
7. Anomie and Apathy: Perceptions of Invisibility 83
8. The Civil Rights Era: Adhering to the Messages from our Past 90
9. Looking Toward the Future:
   Resolving the Issues of Disenfranchisement 94

References 99
Works Consulted 103
Appendix 105
Acknowledgements 107

Thank you Father for giving me the words . . .

To "Big Joyce"—I love you. For the future: Khaliff, Khamall, Kyla, Koran, Khalill and Kaleb. To the inspiration of the JAMAR Institute: James and Margaritte Rogers, and the Trailblazers: Barbara and Ronnie Sr. This work is also dedicated to Dr. Reginald Martin, who always taught me that "Once something is put in ink, it becomes permanent."

PREFACE

The term "Disenfranchisement" is, somewhat, elusive to define. It is ambiguous and used synonymously with terms such as: deprive, destroy and denigrate. This book defines the term as any problematic, inhibiting issue (e.g., learned helplessness, socioeconomic, political non-representation, low self-esteem, and low-leveled aspirations for future prosperity and life) that disconnect individuals from gaining access to educational, economic and social/political prosperity.

The indicators of disenfranchisement are found throughout our everyday environment. Whether we choose to identify them in the actions of a local murder committed by a gang-affiliated, inner-city teenager, or when policymakers choose to ignore the imbrued effects of a decaying community, riddled with such violence, drugs and destruction, that it constrains its citizens as live-in hostages. And, finally, when we can see the regressive, economic effects on a community and/or city—so brutally ignored—that the direct impact to its citizens is measured by a substantial illiteracy rate, which correlates to the economic productivity of that city. It is then, that we must understand that the inherent survival of our society is contingent upon the consistency of our ability to embrace the true responsibility of productive, unselfish change.

Change is hindered when the "powers that be" seek to resolve problematic community issues with "smoke and mirror" tactics. These programs appear and disappear without ever addressing or impacting the root causes. These strategies, while being short-lived and ineffective, can be compared to the effectiveness of applying a band-aid to a severed artery. True change, through the enfranchisement of African Americans, will only occur through the liberation of our society from racism. In order to achieve this, there must be revolution on a national platform. The forthcoming societal revolution (of this millennium) will not, necessarily, be one of turbulence. History has often taught us that when citizens become fatigued with oppression, rebellion is always the product. This effect has been witnessed, in this country, in the events of the Red Summer of 1919, the Montgomery Bus Boycott of 1955, the Detroit and Watts Riots of the 1960s and the Los Angeles Riots of 1992.

The beginning stages of our societal revolution have already begun taking place around our country. As some of our disenfranchised African American male youth begin to afflict irreparable damage to their citizenship, and very lives; their gang involvement, sociopathic behavior, learned helplessness mentality and anomie and apathy set the stage for an unstable future. As the momentum for disenfranchised African American men continues to grow, we, the productive citizen community, internally reverberate the rhetorical question of "Why do our Black, male youth (and some adults) continue to behave with little or no regard for life, authority and consequence?"

In looking to our past, we may begin to understand disenfranchisement, which has been established through a consortium of consistent patterns of ignorance, systematic racism and disregard of the debilitating psychological effects that render its African American victims helpless.

In Letter from Birmingham City Jail, Dr. Martin Luther King, Jr. captured the foundational psyche of Disenfranchised African Americans in a, more than, 300-word sentence that embodied the irreverence and moral disdain felt, both then and now, by socially-conscious African Americans, both since and before this country's inception.

> I guess it is easy for those who have never felt the stinging darts of segregation to say, "Wait." But when you have seen vicious mobs lynch your mothers and fathers at will and drown your sisters and brothers at whim; when you have seen hate-filled

policemen curse, kick, brutalize and even kill your black brothers and sisters with impunity; when you see the vast majority of your twenty million Negro brothers smothering in an airtight cage of poverty in the midst of an affluent society; when you suddenly find your tongue twisted and your speech stammering as you seek to explain to your six-year-old daughter why she can't go to the public amusement park that has just been advertised on television, and see tears welling up in her little eyes when she is told that Funtown is closed to colored children, and see the depressing clouds of inferiority begin to form in her little mental sky, and see her begin to distort her little personality by unconsciously developing a bitterness toward white people; when you have to concoct an answer for a five-year-old son asking in agonizing pathos: "Daddy, why do white people treat colored people so mean?"; when you take a cross-country drive and find it necessary to sleep night after night in the uncomfortable corners of your automobile because no motel will accept you; when you are humiliated day in and day out by nagging signs reading "white" and "colored"; when your first name becomes "nigger" and your middle name becomes "boy" (however old you are) and your last name becomes "John," and when your wife and mother are never given the respected title "Mrs."; when you are harried by day and haunted by night by the fact that you are a Negro, living constantly at tiptoe stance never quite knowing what to expect next, and plagued with inner fears and outer resentments; when you are forever fighting a degenerating sense of "nobodiness"; then you will understand why we find it difficult to wait.

This book was written to expose the true and consistent problem of disenfranchisement, and its detrimental effects on African American men. The secondary intent of this work was to provide a blueprint for policy reform. The suggested methods provided to permanently resolve the genocidal effects of disenfranchisement have proven successful in liberating disenfranchised men and communities.

Resolving the plague of disenfranchisement does not require radical demonstration. Rather, it will require a consistent equilibrium of properly-written policies and implementation that address the issues of our failing communities. Grass root community organizations must be enacted that dynamically engage our troubled youth and expose them to thought-provoking, progressive atmospheres, which lead to a better quality of life; and a resurgence of cohesive African-American men/women relationships. The latter demonstrates the true derivative of any society.

We must, at some point, begin to isolate the variables that promote the genocidal continuance of the disenfranchisement of African Americans. This book provides innovative strategies and techniques that seek to negate and reverse what some consider to be inexorable.

Consequently, we are faced with the moral imperative to embrace the unknown. Win, lose, or draw, we must be prepared to accept the consequences of change. In the end . . .

> *"You're either part of the solution or you're part of the problem."*
>
> —Eldridge Cleaver

Definition of Key Terms

The following were operationally defined as they relate to this study:

1. *Anomia or Anomie:* Associated with apathy. Mentality associated with depression and feelings of hopelessness for future progress (Robinson, Shaver, & Wrightsman, 1991).
2. *Disenfranchisement:* Defined and described as problematic, inhibiting issues (e.g., learned helplessness, socioeconomic, political non-representation, low self-esteem and low-leveled aspirations for future economic prosperity and life) that preclude individuals from gaining access to educational, economic and social/political success.
3. *Economic Disenfranchisement:* The lack of legitimate dollars made, spent and invested for the advancement of self, family and community.
4. *Educational Disenfranchisement:* The lack of investment into human capital to make learning and instruction significant and beneficial for disadvantaged youth.
5. *Learned Helplessness:* Defeatist attitudes developed that inhibit ability to learn beyond a level of difficulty.
6. *Racism:* Any discriminatory action inflicted by one race of people against another. These actions are usually generated by stereotypical beliefs that one race of people is superior to the other (Kozol, 1991).
7. *Social/Political Disenfranchisement:* The loss or decline of rights and/or privileges. This includes the rights of citizenship, such as the right to vote (Reed, 2003).
8. *Systemic/Systematic Discrimination:* The continuous cycle of racist behavior and attitudes carried on over a period of time (e.g., non-allowance of African Americans into Ph.D./Ed.D. programs because of color).

CHAPTER 1

Defining Disenfranchisement in the African American Community

Civil rights had achieved what it set out to achieve—franchise, the end of statutory racial discrimination. It was a triumph. However, some of the more difficult questions, such as economic equity, basic attitudes, and the empowerment of the inner cities, remained. They were left on the table after 1965.

Claude A. Clegg III
Associate professor of history
Indiana University at Bloomington

Researchers have suggested that African Americans have been victimized by racism more than any other racial group in the United States. According to Schansberg (1996), racism is the infliction of an attitude characterized by superior beliefs, presuppositions and biases of one racial group against another. Schansberg also indicates that, " . . . the greatest problems with discrimination against racial minorities have been caused or perpetuated by government, for example, slavery, police brutality, the Dred Scott decision, public school segregation, Jim Crow laws, Davis-Bacon laws . . ." (p. 28).

Those who believe that racism is currently practiced in this country also believe that systematic racist practices have become normalized (Kozol, 1991). According to Haskins (1973), systemic racism is identified by the superior attitudes, egos and stereotypes that are enforced over a period of time by one racial group against another. Haskins discusses the idea of systemic racism as it applies to the education of today's African-American youth when he states the following:

> It is plain from the evidence that education for Black children is no longer merely inadequate; it is now almost hopeless . . . The school was successful with masses of illiterate Irish, Jews, and other white ethnic groups . . . Why are the classrooms dysfunctional now when the majority of students . . . are Black (p. 9).

To the socially conscious, it is already known that African Americans have been exposed to a longstanding experience with systemic racism and discrimination. With the slave trade of Africans beginning in 1555, to the signing of the Civil Rights Act, in 1964, African Americans have consistently been immersed in a state of peril. Due to this history, the mentality and behavior of disenfranchisement has been the result.

Research has also suggested that through the racist practices of some Americans; schools, homes, and communities, mainly catering to African Americans, have " . . . failed black (African American) children . . . in the most fundamental ways possible by not providing for their needs" (Kunjufu, 1998, p. 12). Haskins also introduces other educational indicators of disenfranchisement. These include the impeding actions of; learned helplessness and the mislabeling of children through placement in special education. This is most notably recognized in the misdiagnosis of Attention Deficit Disorder (ADD) and Attention Deficit Hyperactivity Disorder (ADHD).

Daniels (2001), editor of the Urban League's publication, *The State of Black America 2001*, provides further commentary on the inhibiting nature of systemic racism against blacks by pointing out that, "Black people know the serious strains of racism—the violent kind that threatens our very lives; the institutional kind that systematically works to deny us (African Americans) opportunity . . ." (p. 11). Daniels' statement expresses systemic racism as a precursor to disenfranchisement. One of the genocidal effects of systemic racism includes the mentality known as *self-fulfilling prophecy*.

This disabling mentality is where one develops the self concept of what he/she is programmed to believe by another. In the instance where a child is programmed (by the parent or guardian) to believe that he/she is mentally inept or incorrigible, it is then that the child may be likely to develop or function with a learning and/or emotional disability. These disabilities, coupled with the onslaught of learned helplessness, create pathways to a negative return. This major deterrent, which currently faces the population of America's disenfranchised African Americans, (males especially) in fact, perpetuate destructive and genocidal life choices.

A variety of research defines the impact of disenfranchisement, but mainly as a lack/deprivity of political policies, educational programs and social mobility. Researchers have identified that African American men who suffer from disenfranchisement can exhibit certain characteristics (indicators) such as low-level future aspirations, low educational attainment, and an apathetic outlook on life, personal finances and political policies. These characteristics lead to a deconstruction of the African American community that manifests itself in various, derogatory forms.

Specifically, disenfranchisement in African-American communities can be attributed to the ineffectiveness or lack of revision of disenfranchising policies. For example, if we analyze President Lyndon B. Johnson's Economic Improvement Act, Welfare Reform Law of 1966, and the many recidivism programs that have been implemented across the country, which supposedly seek to rehabilitate its prisoners, we would find that the initial political intent has now deviated from its impact. It is believed that policies will only be changed, once disenfranchised African Americans begin to question and contest laws that are unfairly thwarted upon them. Nonetheless, passive revolution will only be brought about through education.

Three areas where disenfranchisement occurs, particularly for African Americans, are in the educational, economic, and social/political arenas. Educational disenfranchisement can be identified by the concept of learned helplessness, a consequence referring to a person's development of defeatist attitudes toward challenging educational endeavors (Shields, 1997). Learned helplessness, coupled with poor perceptions about systemic racism, is not only widespread, but is mainly undetected by individuals of whom the barbarism of systemic racism is perpetrated against (West, 1993). Economic disenfranchisement is identified by the lack of economic resources/opportunities that can improve quality of life, life expectancy, life chances and social mobility. Finally, social/political disenfranchisement can be evidenced by the number of African Americans, specifically men, who have lost voting rights (Reed, 2003). All indicators of disenfranchisement are prevalent in large, urban ghettoized communities (Kozol, 1991).

The result, according to Kunjufu (1982), is a continuation of the injustices promulgated through non-empathetic, narcissistic policymakers and educators who systematically promote a repetitive cycle of economic, educational and social/political disenfranchisement. These actions "trickle down" through generations of African Americans causing significant impact to their ability to reproduce or become a contributing member of society (Reed, 2003). Reed further promotes his theory in the supportive commentary:

> Unavailable to help build economics among deteriorated black social structures. Once gone, our castrated black men never come back to us. There's no longer even a guise of rehabilitation in current penal philosophy. After all: rehabilitate for what? To go back into an economy which has no jobs or hope (p. 3)?

The Influence of Anomie

According to Durkheim (1933), anomie exists when social and/or moral norms are confused, unclear or simply not present. Durkheim explains that this lack of norms, or pre-accepted limits on behavior in a society, lead to deviant behavior. Giddens (1972) indicates his belief of how to counteract anomie in the following:

> ... The state of anomie is impossible whenever interdependent organs are sufficiently in contact and sufficiently extensive. If they are close to each other, they are readily aware, in every situation, of the need which they have of one-another, and consequently they have an active and permanent feeling of mutual dependence [excerpt from *The Division of Labor in Society*] (p. 184).

The impact of educational, economic and social/political disenfranchisement on some African American men has resulted in their anomie. The city of Memphis, Tennessee served as the premier research location for this book. Pursuant to the research, it was hypothesized that disenfranchised, African-American men existed in abundance. Whether by choice or design, disenfranchisement remains an interwoven facet of the city of Memphis, Tennessee.

Memphis is not the only city affected by the cruel barbarism of disenfranchisement. Other cities, where disenfranchisement is prevalent include: East St. Louis, Illinois; Waukegan, Illinois; and other places throughout this country where equitable economics, education and social-politicism, blatantly seem to exclude African Americans.

The problem is that certain municipalities, in America, are a bedlam for educational, economic and social/political adversity toward African American men. This book empathetically describes the long term effects of disenfranchisement toward African American men and how to identify a high concentration of its existence in certain cities. Furthermore, the phenomenon of educational, economic and social/political disenfranchisement, experienced by African American men, ultimately results in a co-dependence of anomie and apathy.

Macleod (1987), an ethnographer, conducted a pilot study investigating both the cause and effects of disenfranchisement experienced by low socioeconomic youth. His work, as well as others, influenced the design of this study. In Macleod's book entitled *Ain't no makin' it: leveled aspirations in a low-income neighborhood* an analysis on black and white male lifestyles and their perceptions of life in a low-income neighborhood was conducted. For this study, disenfranchisement was specifically researched in an identical fashion; however, black men, 18 to 35 years old, represented the only demographic of persons investigated.

According to Comer and Poussaint (1992), "Since the end of the civil rights movement, the struggle for racial equality has diminished" (pp. 8-9). As a result, an improved quality of life for African Americans has been experienced in "fair standards," such as voting rights, desegregation of schools and affirmative action. Today, these diminished standards have matriculated inversely proportional perceptions, where some African Americans have developed a false sense of security, believing that both racism (systemic) and disenfranchisement do not exist (West, 1993).

The successful analysis of disenfranchisement in African Americans produces an arousal of conscious awareness (Kunjufu, 1982). This awareness focuses on the creation of both equitable economic, social and educational standards that improves both life chances and expectancies for African Americans, both before and beyond the 18 to 35 age range. Furthermore, African American consciousness has sensitized some policymakers on both the conditions of disenfranchisement, and the data that could be used to promote both policy changes and reductions in the number of disenfranchised African Americans.

Investigative Research Questions

The following research questions were investigated in this study:

1. What are the educational characteristics that lead to the disenfranchisement of African Americans, specifically males between the ages of 18 and 35?

2. What are the economic characteristics of disenfranchisement in African Americans, specifically men, between the ages of 18 and 35?
3. What are the social/political characteristics of disenfranchisement in African American males, specifically those between the ages of 18 and 35?
4. What is the relationship between the demographic variables, educational, economic and social/political characteristics of disenfranchisement for African American males, specifically those between the ages of 18 and 35, and anomie?

Supportive research offered by authors, Cornell West and Kwanzaa Kunjufu suggests that perhaps there has been an oversight in the reform of both education and economics in the African American community. This oversight insinuates the existence of a gap in the implementation of political services and policies that could, potentially, improve society. Additionally, both educational and economic reform policies have, simply, failed disenfranchised African Americans, specifically men. This is based on the existence of the derogatory characteristics of disenfranchisement (indicators) exemplified by African Americans, especially in men, 18 to 35 years of age.

The forthcoming research, has analyzed the characteristics associated with African American male disenfranchisement. Through the identification of these characteristics, communities can develop strategic plans to eradicate this plague, which has destroyed African Americans of both the past and present. Consequently, without the implementation of a true resolve, the future multitude of unborn disenfranchised African Americans is predisposed to the same course of action.

CHAPTER 2

Educational Disenfranchisement

> *Learned helplessness is the giving up reaction, the quitting response that follows from the belief that whatever you do doesn't matter.*
>
> **Martin Seligman**
> **Learned Optimism**

As the fundamental definition of disenfranchisement has been established, exploits of educational disenfranchisement must be analyzed. Disenfranchisement has been previously defined as, " . . . some problematic, inhibiting issues that disempower African Americans from gaining access to social/political, educational and economic success." Educational disenfranchisement is defined as the lack of investment into human capital, where learning and instruction are made significant/beneficial for disadvantaged youth (Kozol, 1991).

Analysis of the three types of disenfranchisement has provided this study with depth; however, in order to truly engage the concept of educational disenfranchisement, clarity of its indicators must be established.

Defining Educational Disenfranchisement

To disenfranchise means to withdraw certification or to terminate a franchise. This definition assists with the understanding of policy impact. This deprives people of their humanistic, political, educational, socioeconomic or common rights. Moreover, the implementation of disenfranchisement manifests barriers that restrict one's ability to successfully counteract.

Disenfranchisement is an ambiguous term with multiple interpretations that can be characterized by the destructive plight affecting African American men. Additionally, it can be viewed as an unforeseen force that denies the opportunity for one to positively promote or achieve one's true potential for ascertaining educational, economic and/or social/political stability (Reed, 2003).

Assumption About the Subjects

Urban, African-American, mid-southern communities, especially in Memphis, Tennessee, have been and are currently being destroyed from the inside out, due to a lack of black, educational, economic and social/political participation (Anderson, 2002). This lack of participation is an underlying cause of disenfranchisement. Black, inner-city youth experience daily, genocidal lifestyles (Billson, 1992) through the lack of economic investment (i.e., re-circulation and participation of black capital). This ultimately prevents the prosperity of community (Freedman, 1993).

Genocide is socially and physically committed on the streets of African American, inner-city communities through the perpetration of homicides, gang activity, drug sales/use (Tukufu, 1997). These deviant activities always lead to death or incarceration. This cycle prevents disenfranchised, inner-city African Americans from reproducing themselves (i.e., genocide). Once men have been extracted from the equation of family, on a massive scale, black communities are left devoid, and black families jilted—without the presence of a father (West, 1993).

Evidence of this effect can be witnessed in the policy of the welfare act, as defined by the Aid to Families and Dependent Children Act (AFDC). Family (i.e., welfare recipient) is defined to include only one parent with a child and/or children. Socially, this policy sabotages the black family/community for failure because without the presence of both parents, black families/communities are left incomplete (McWhirter, McWhirter, McWhirter, & McWhirter, 1993).

The practice of extracting the father from the family has multiplied over the years, creating a domino effect. This effect manifests itself in disenfranchised black children and can be observed through actions, such as: inferiority complexes, internalized anger and low self-concept and esteem. These feelings, left unaddressed, ultimately manifest in the form of violence, drug use, deviant behavior and a sedentary attitude toward school/life; thereby, perpetuating the cycle of disenfranchisement (Neal, 2003). These indicators of disenfranchisement are most commonly witnessed in African American youth from elementary through young adulthood (Kozol, 1992). In the efforts to improve the African American community, riddled with the negative effects of disenfranchisement, the underlying causes (i.e., indicative factors) must be identified and prevented.

Genocide within the African-American community is witnessed through the existence of educational disenfranchisement. Common practices of educational disenfranchisement are committed in some classrooms of low-performing schools located primarily in inner-city communities. These communities typically have a majority black student body, who are economically disadvantaged. Educational disenfranchisement can also be recognized in schools that have a predominately white student body, with a disproportionate number of black children, specifically males, who are wrongly assigned to special education and/or unfairly retained because of discriminatory practices (Ladner, 2004 & Owo, 2004). Additionally, disenfranchised black children are consistently misdiagnosed with Attention Deficit Hyperactivity Disorder (ADHD).

Ultimately, these discriminatory practices negatively impact the lives of disenfranchised African American men and their communities. This effect can be witnessed in many aspects of everyday life. Specifically, it can be seen in such areas as the African American unemployment rate, number of African American households at or below the poverty level (The Civil Rights Project, 2001), African American illiteracy, secondary cohort dropout and graduation rates, infant mortality and attrition rates.

Simply, it is a moral imperative that we understand the importance of education and how it permeates one's ability to succeed economically throughout life. Despite argument and opposition of the importance of education, disenfranchised citizens must know that these practices will continue the destruction of the black community, if the lack of community participation (e.g., voting, community activism and education) remains in its current state.

Educational Disenfranchisement: Learned Helplessness

Researchers Reed (2003) and Kunjufu (1982) define the dimensions of disenfranchisement. Kunjufu hypothesizes that educational disenfranchisement is an inhibitor for African Americans, especially men, when attempting to empower themselves for success. This theory is supported by Barton and Pillai (1997) who state, " . . . racial prejudices and discrimination shut out a large portion of the African Americans from both educational and job opportunities. Thus, abject poverty among African Americans is largely a result of widespread discrimination against African-Americans" (p. 9). Agreement with this statement produces mixed feelings because of the following reasons:

1. Many Americans do not believe that racism still exists
2. Many Americans judge poor African Americans by the success of other ethnic groups (e.g., Asian immigrants) (Schansberg, 1996).

Disenfranchised African American men were identified as men, under the age 40, who were mislabeled through special education, represent the majority of incarcerated males, and have developed a tolerance for their destitute economic surroundings (Haskins, 1973). This developed tolerance introduces another indicator of educational disenfranchisement—the mentality of *learned helplessness*. *Learned Helplessness* is defined as the "general expectation that one cannot control important events (mainly educationally related) leading to lowered persistence, motivation, self-esteem and initiative" (BlueRider.com). This mentality, possessed by many young, disenfranchised African Americans, is believed to be prompted by the substandard educational services provided in disenfranchised African American communities.

Some researchers believe that education is regarded as the single most important factor for stabilizing America's economy (Schansberg, 1996). If education is prescribed for a sound and productive economic future for America, then it must be implemented in an equitable fashion for all Americans. There is no right to education written in the U.S. Constitution; however, education, of some sort, whether formal or informal, is necessary to obtain the finer points of living (Fuller, 1999).

Education is a highly regarded resource because of its potential to supply trained human capital (Schansberg, 1996). Yet, there are hindrances plaguing both secondary and post-secondary education that perpetuate the cycle of disenfranchisement in low-income African American communities. The mentality of *learned helplessness* is shared by some African Americans of disenfranchised families. Many researchers feel that this mentality leads to the demise of future growth and productivity in the African American household, because once a family has this mentality, it is highly unlikely that they will rid themselves of it (Gordon, 1996).

Understanding *learned helplessness* is detrimental to African Americans because it perpetuates disenfranchisement in the form of genocide. The genocidal aspect of learned helplessness transcends generations from parent to child. Learned helplessness can be inflicted upon children by parents and/or teachers (Shields, 1997). This problem perpetuates when the child creates a buffer that consists of deteriorated self-confidence, and/or the belief that success is unattainable (Shields, 1997).

Once developed, this mentality causes one to be lost academically. Upon graduation from high school (if this occurs), the young adult enters society with a warped perception of success, a low self-esteem, and an inferiority complex (Shields, 1997). At this point, it becomes very easy for the young adult to accept his/her role in society as a social deviant, an unskilled worker or as a welfare recipient, completely relying on "the system" to sustain life—regardless of the quality.

Nationally acclaimed motivational speaker, Crystal Kuykendall (1991), provides shocking statistics about educationally disenfranchised, black youth in the following:

1. Black youth today have a 1 in 684 chance of becoming a physicist
2. Black youth today have a 1 in 377 chance of becoming a doctor
3. Black youth today have a 1 in 99 chance of becoming a teacher
4. Black youth today have a 1 in 20 chance of being killed.
5. Black youth today have a 1 in 3 chance of becoming a prisoner.

According to Kuykendall, these are the statistics that black children face all over the country, "before they even go to school." With the many problems facing disenfranchised black children, at some point, we must consider the ramifications of what happens when children "slip through the cracks." The increase in gang activity over the years should be a constant reminder to us that society is failing our children.

Everyday the media reminds us, through the negative reports on deviant children, that education is not the primary focus for our children. One such individual, Kody Scott, [Sanyika Shakur] reported his experiences with disenfranchisement, which led him astray down a pathway of deviance. In his book, *Monster: The Autobiography of an L.A. Gang Member,* Kody reported the following:

> Looking back now it's quite amusing to remember how proud I was and how superior I felt next to Joe Johnson (school mate and

gang rival). I first sensed my radical departure from childhood when I was suspended a month before graduation, driven home by Mr. Smotherman, the principal, and not allowed to go on the grad-class outing for flashing a gang sign on the school panorama picture . . . I was completely sold on becoming a gang member . . . As our graduation activities bore on, my disinterest an annoyance at its silliness escalated. I was eager to get home to the "*hood*" and to meet my moral obligation to my new set of friends (Shakur, 1993, pp. 3-4).

At some point, gang activity must become the subject of study for problems plaguing education. If educational interest is not upheld in the household or community; peer pressures of gang activity, outward resistance from discriminatory behavior or inner noise (i.e., learned helplessness) becomes the expected norm. Society must be prepared to accept and rival the consequences that come as a result of losing children to disenfranchisement. These consequences that are inflicted upon our youth include incarceration, loss of voting rights, *anomie,* and death. Moreover, the consequence for allowing disenfranchisement to engulf our children directly affects society by making productive citizens into victims (McCall, 1994).

McCall furthers his point by recalling a conversation held with a former schoolmate in the following:

> . . . I ran into Holt, who lived around my way and often swung with the fellas and me. He had a pocketful of cash, even though he had quit school and was unemployed. I asked him, "Yo, man, what you been into?" "Me and my partner kick in cribs and make a killin'. You oughta come go with us sometimes . . ." I hooked school one day, went with them, and pulled my first B&E (Breaking and Entering) (p. 98).

Another such way that policymakers support the disenfranchisement of African Americans is through the lack of effective educational policy. Today, the largest educational policy in this country is the No Child Left Behind Law (NCLB). This educational policy is directly correlated with economics because its implementation deals largely with money. The intended purpose of this federal subsidy is to provide an equitable playing field for impoverished families who, otherwise, are jaded from the true goal of education—to create productive citizens to receive the standard academic prerequisites in preparation for postsecondary life or education.

Two areas of emphasis for this policy include Title I, which is used for economically disadvantaged students, and Title II, which is used for the recruitment, professional development, and retention of highly qualified teachers. Consequently, the public money appropriated by Congress, is being reported "insufficient" by many school districts around the country. With our country already experiencing economic shortfall, public schools have the common denominator most affected by this—children.

Sidebar issues (e.g., budget shortfall, legislative ambiguity, etc.) directly and indirectly affect the primary educational/legislative intention of NCLB. This intention is to make both elementary and secondary education equitable and attainable for all students (Cowan & Manasevit, 2002). A major sidebar issue compromising educational dollars is the War in Iraq, which takes about 80+ billion dollars from the U.S. budget (Muhammad, 2003). This is not to say that dollars for the war are misappropriated; however, the public should understand the inversely proportional relationship of pulling dollars from one cause to support another (i.e., dollars for the war deplete dollars for public education).

The understanding of policy and the policymaking process is key to understanding the possibilities of change in disenfranchised communities. Policy dictates rules and regulations, which allow for the continuation of both democracy and the homeostasis of business, congress and citizenship. The methodology of policy, which was used in the establishment of an efficient society, may now be responsible for its compromise. In this vein, we must seek to understand the following:

1. The steps involved in the policy process
2. The consequences experienced by organizations and people who do not understand the process of policy implementation.

The increase in technology, information processing, and the importing and exporting of goods and services renders America as one of the most economically affluent, yet most political nations in the world. Due to certain inequitable policies, both educational and economic prosperity has been deemed unattainable by disenfranchised African American men.

In addition to the derogatory policies causing disenfranchisement, the inclusion of people (especially those negatively affected by implementation) is often overlooked during the policymaking process. Without people there is no policy; without policy, there is no organization; without organization, there is no progress.

CHAPTER 3

Understanding the Policymaking Process to end Disenfranchisement

"A policy is a temporary creed liable to be changed, but while it holds good it has got to be pursued with apostolic zeal."

Mahatma Gandhi

Currently, there is a growing tension, in the political arena, that now exists because people, who were once without knowledge of the policy process, now possess an understanding of it. Furthermore, these individuals are now becoming advisors for policymakers and advocacy groups.

This knowledge could prove to be the change in government if disenfranchised African Americans effectively used the knowledge of policy and the powers of persuasion and organization (Jones, 1997).

Policy is controversial. This holds especially true when a word has multiple definitions. Queensland defines policy as "A course of action or inaction chosen by public authorities to address a given problem or interrelated set of problems" (Queensland, 2001, p. 1). Queensland adds that policy is also " . . . a set of interrelated decisions taken by a political actor or group of actors concerning the selection of goals and the means of achieving them within a specified situation" (2001, p. 1). The final definition adds, "Public policy is a choice made by government to undertake some course of action" (Queensland, 2001, p. 1).

Analyzing disenfranchisement should prompt understanding of policy among African American men, particularly those who are disenfranchised. Although evident in government, communities, schools and churches; there must be a movement of individuals who are concerned with impacting a productive change for generations, both current and future, to rescue them from abject poverty, ignorance and death.

The Queensland Policy Handbook provides understanding of policymaking that does not exclude individuals or organizations, in service to communities, from the process:

> Public policy is both an art and a craft. It is an art because it requires insight, creativity, and imagination in identifying societal problems and describing them, in devising public policies that might alleviate them, and then in finding out whether these policies end up making things better or worse (Queensland, 2001, p. 2).

Implementation of policy does not mandate acceptance by all who are affected. Ambiguity of policy and poor public perception demonstrate the discrepancies in policymaking, which continue to supply states and plague municipalities with scrutiny. Moreover, this scrutiny prescribes to the travesties of both disorganization and distrust possessed by the disenfranchised public.

Control is the key ingredient in the implementation of policy (Jones, 1997). More important than the idea of control are the persons or entities who have it. Many believe legislators to be the culprits behind policy problems, such as the major policy issues (i.e., direct and indirect) involving the regressive tax base issue in some states. "Public policy is whatever governments choose to do or not to do" (Queensland, 2001, p. 2).

Currently, Tennessee does not have a State income tax. Conversely, the state continues to generate a portion of its revenue by having one of the nation's highest sales tax. This policy proves acceptable for individuals who make either, a substantial and/or adequate salary, partially affected by sales tax. Moreover, inequitable policies ensure individuals, who generate a diminished salary, (i.e., at or below poverty level) exposure to a high tax rate. This affects a larger percentage of their income. This effect is significant to the point, where children do not eat, or where adequate medication is not purchased. This attack on our impoverished must be eliminated. This will stop the loss of life.

Public distrust generated from policymaking is phenomenal. This is largely due to hidden agendas and campaigns, which are perceived by the public to be owned by politicians. This presents itself as a problem to schools because, ultimately, it is the children who suffer. "People who control schools and school districts don't really care whether you picket, or whether you change superintendents. You can do all of that. People in power start listening when you start talking about control of the money" (Fuller, 1999, p. 8).

The perceived correlation between legislators and abuse of policy control is widespread. This notion is supported by the belief that power is regulated by influence. Ideally, this segues the significance of including disenfranchised individuals (e.g., African American men) in the policymaking process.

Leadership is the ability of an individual or group to take control of or represent an organization with success, synergy and charisma. An individual with such control would have to possess many qualities such as: style, vision, intellect, and articulation. Although more commonly referred to as an actor, lobbyists achieve power through the persuasion and support of an organization capable of favorably presenting itself to a legislative body.

The spokesperson must reflect the organization's character. Furthermore, he/she must support the goal of the organization by acquiring mass followership. This practice retains integrity by keeping the focus on the large machine of the legislative process. Legislators who only insist on hearing organizations with the powers of persuasion truly commit the crime of perpetuating the status quo. It is this crime, which continues the disenfranchisement of African American men and their communities.

Control, for an unempathetic policymaker, is perhaps the most important reason as to why policymakers retain their positions. This underlying agenda for some policymakers is used as a means to exercise control of community and its members. In order to counteract this control, communities must learn to embrace the problems of its people. "When people become involved, the issues are identified and then alternatives are considered" (GIS, 2001, p. 1).

Other issues associated with control include money. "The bureaucracy of public education is perpetuated by dollars or lack thereof" (Davis Interview, 2001). This implies that hindrances, caused by the lack of money, may inhibit the educational process, which proves economically catastrophic for our non-educated youth, later in their lives. This disenfranchisement is due to the lack of investment in human capital. One solution to the hindrances that prevent successful implementation of policy is the understanding of its process and players (i.e., implementation of, who is responsible, etc.).

The Political Process

The cyclic process of policy is not difficult to understand. However, its ease of comprehension is bombarded by its difficulty of implementation (easier said than done). This process is best explained in the following figure provided by Charles O. Jones (1997):

Figure 1: Framework for Policy Analysis

- Definition of Problem
- Problem to Government
- Action in Government
- Government to Problems
- Program to Government

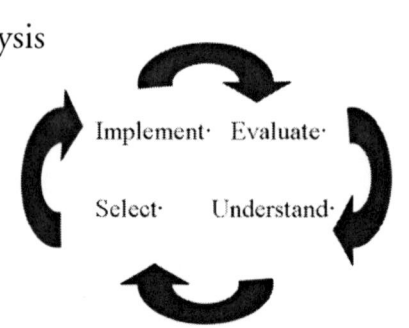

Implementation of these steps is cumbersome, yet necessary in the legitimizing of programs. These steps are also known as the procurement of policy. The first step of policymaking is to identify the problem that requires attention. Researcher Charles O. Jones, refers to this process as being " . . . subject to mixed signals" (Jones, 1997, p. 35).

The second step entails the proposal, which is developed to treat the problem. Jones states, "It may involve elaborate institutional processes for getting agreement" (p. 35). It is here, in the second phase, that the political process is recognized and; therefore, should be handled with caution. "Some policies never make it out of proposal stage, due to many indifferences" (Davis, 2001).

Third, the policy proposal is shifted through the decision-making process. This phase of policymaking involves critical analysis of the proposal, such as a building of a larger support base, "a search for analogies and precedents" (Jones, 1997, p. 35), and anticipation of bargaining and expectation complexes.

The fourth step in policy making, which assists in resolving the issues of disenfranchisement for African Americans, involves an obtuse and indirect policy result from policymakers. The final two stages in policy development include the implementation and evaluation of policy (respectively). According to Jones (1997), "Even bad programs develop a supporting clientele" (p. 35).

In an interview with Milton Bradley, spokesman for Tennesseans for Fair Taxation, Bradley stated that a major inhibiting factor in American policymaking is "Finding legislators who will listen and offer their continued support is the hardest part" (Davis Interview, 2001). This problem has prevented and prolonged valid issues from reaching change agents, both in government and with the public. According to Jones (1997), this is why organizations (e.g., grassroots organizations, advocacy groups, think tanks, etc.) consider the charisma of the spokesperson, when seeking a representative, who can effectively transcend the cause of the organization. This person must be able to conduct him/herself in a manner that parallels the goals of the organization. This "actor" must also possess the ability to be persuasive in their rhetoric.

Figure 1 provided the conceptual framework behind policy implementation; however, figure 2 provides a more in-depth analysis. Figure 2 explains additional steps that provide more detail to the general concept of the policy cycle. It is here that Charles O. Jones (1997) expresses his research in the following:

Figure 2: The American way of policy making

>Problem Identified → Proposal Development → Decision Making Process → Program Results: Obtuse, Unintegrated → Implementation → Evaluation: Justify and Expansion

Figure 2 provides all steps involved in the policy implementation process (i.e., lobbying and the conclusive aftermath). Ultimately, it is imperative for organizations and government to remember that the responsibilities of policy implementation do not lie with one person, but with the numbers of dedicated constituents. Through these efforts, full attention and support of legislators can be obtained. This ultimately results in creating a greater society for the individual, family and business.

The Suffering of Children

To understand the nature of bureaucracy and policy, one must be exposed to its tangible essence, through real-world experience. Policy has mandated that most public schools in America obtain a majority of its funding from taxes imposed on local property. Although some may not see the potential problems associated with this situation, there is indeed a major problem in this scenario—an inequitable one.

"A typically wealthy suburb . . . draws upon a larger tax base in proportion to its student population than a city occupied by thousands of poor people" (Kozol, 1991, p. 55). In such cases, indigent people are penalized for being poor, while more affluent communities can provide economic stability. These real-life issues should alert society to everyday problems that require policy revision.

Unfortunately, the disenfranchised, indigent community is prohibited from organizing and selecting a charismatic actor to champion their crusade. States and municipalities with high sales taxes create a regressive tax base for the indigent. This ultimately contributes to the lasting economic hardship of disenfranchised African Americans. Conversely, the inadequacy of state and municipal budgets, due to a lack of revenue, causes for the inadequate provision of services to provide a better quality of life for its citizens. As a result, there are now organizations that seek to educate the general public on matters of state tax policy (e.g., www.yourtax.org).

The question of who suffers is evident; therefore, a true solution to inequitable policy implementation lies somewhere in the midst of a utopian bureaucracy (if such a place exists). According to Dr. Howard Fuller, "Our children are out here dying. Our children need us and the only way that we are going to be able to help them is to give them a level of power that they do not currently have" (Fuller, 1999, p. 8).

Perhaps Fuller suggests that by empowering our children, we also empower a community of future generations. Dr. Howard Fuller and Jonathan Kozol (author of *Savage Inequalities*), feel that a political change is necessary for the preservation of youth. Kozol (1991) further states, "If it doesn't matter (money for schools), cancel it for everybody. Don't give to them, deny it to us, then ask us to believe that it is not significant" (p. 118). Additionally, Dr. Howard Fuller supplies the following comment on implementing change in politics: " . . . large bureaucracies do not change unless you can materially affect the people who work in them" (Fuller, 1999, p. 8).

Changes

The effects of policy are felt by those who take advantage of the democratic process, as well as by those who are on the receiving end of disenfranchisement. America's economy was created and maintained from the methodology of policy and politics. "Political economy . . . proposes two distinct objects: first, to provide a plentiful revenue or subsistence for the people, or more properly to enable them to provide . . . for themselves" (Smith, 1880, p. 1).

This insight from the past should assist in regulating policy for the future. If policy was built on the premise of people, then it should retain its status today. If a fear of compromised position exists, then it does in the minds of legislators, who have kept the policy implementation process away from the people.

Some legislators should consider the potential dangers that their compromises have brought to the policy implementation process. Nonetheless, changes are becoming more prevalent with increased legislative confrontations prompted by those who are aware of and unafraid to challenge legislators on their past and/or current indiscretions. Perhaps government should consider a redefining of its criteria on the acceptance and rejection of policies, especially those that create disenfranchisement.

There are some organizations looking to take on the big machine of legislation to ensure their martyr status. This casts policymaking into a trendy light. Adversely, lobbyists/special interest groups with the right combination of capital, charisma, and support can almost initiate change at an "at will" basis.

An example of "at will" policy implementation includes the charter school movement (i.e., the passing of state charter school law) in Tennessee. After five years of lobbying momentum, relationship building and the securing of the proper charismatic players, Tennessee charter law was brought into existence. According to proponents of the law, competition provided by charter schools would prompt/motivate low-performing school districts to improve. This belief, scrutinized by charter opponents, had validity. According to reports by the U.S. Department of Education, "Every district in our study made changes in district education and/or district operations that they attributed to charter schools" (Berryhill, 2001, p. 1).

Power

The implementation of policy is based on power. The government's ability to pass or reject policy shows the sovereign power of policymaking. This power must be redistributed in an equitable fashion that allows every individual to benefit. In order for this to happen, the infrastructure of legislation may have to endure a reconstruction.

This poses a problem for government. The concern is that if power is compromised, then perhaps it can be lost. The ideal of overhauling the policymaking process is suggested in the statement, "A high degree of public access allows people to move in and upset the most orderly and rational plans" (Jones, 1997, p. 33). Jones suggests the possible fear factor as an explanation for harsh, inequitable policies that promote disenfranchisement. Additionally, it is believed that " . . . power is something possessed by 'the rulers,' which enables their rule and, in principle has to be undone so as to provide a more equitable context in which people can equally "negotiate" how resources are allocated" (Popekewitz, 2000, p. 15).

The problems discussed relate to the many difficulties endured via policy implementation. Whether the problems are experienced in education or elsewhere, the fact remains that problems with policy exist.

Both current and future productive members in disenfranchised communities must be educated on policy framework and its cyclical process (figure 1). The empowering of a community does not always occur with money, it can also take place with the correct dissemination of information. This idea is exemplified in the statement that "A little bit of knowledge is a dangerous thing."

Fuller provides a final opinion toward educational injustices prompted by policy infractions that warrant the attention of legislators when he states the following:

> The problem in America is not choice; it's who has it. Every one of us who has money is already able to make certain choices. The only people who can't are low-income parents who we force to stay in schools that the teachers who teach in the schools wouldn't have their children in (Fuller, 1999, p. 8).

In conclusion, policy implementation must not be viewed as the problem. Moreover, the problem is with people, (citizens and legislators) who abuse the policymaking process or disregard the repercussions of, sometimes, biased or influenced decisions. "Policy (or the implementation of) is not a challenge when doing the right thing for people" (Davis, 2001). Perhaps somewhere along the way, some of our legislators have forgotten that.

Systemic Racism: A Deterrent to Social Mobility

The systemic racist practices, imposed by welfare policies and other institutions in this country, (i.e., schools, financial institutions) have been unfairly thwarted upon poor African American communities (Kozol, 1992). This infliction has contributed to the destruction of the African American community through genocide. Genocidal practices have destroyed the spirits of many hopeful African American youth, who have sought the pathway to social mobility through post-secondary education (Kunjufu, 1991). Patterns of instability in impoverished, African American neighborhoods have been perpetuated thorough mediums of learned helplessness amongst African American students (e.g., middle and high school). Evidence of this exists in behaviors, such as poor perceptions of self and future socioeconomic success (Bender & Leone, 1991).

These irreparable damages to society's future infrastructure have led many African Americans to believe that the "American Dream" is unattainable (Bender & Leone, 1991). Some formerly disenfranchised African Americans have sought enfranchisement through education; however, the dilemma facing today's African American students hoping to attend college is systemic racism. According to authors Bender and Leone, "Racism and bigotry are back on campus with a vengeance" (Bender & Leone, 1991, p. 58).

Disenfranchisement in the African American community is a continuous paradigm. The problem associated with this phenomenon is that people who live disenfranchised lives, hardly ever know it. It was believed that through this research and identification of characteristics associated with disenfranchisement that, perhaps, African American men, would, someday, identify and recognize the crippling effects of this plague. Researchers can only speculate when disenfranchisement actually began affecting the African American community. However, those who can actually identify its characteristics, can unmistakably link its continuous debilitating effect on the people, institutions and communities that fall prey to its destructive grasp.

Summary

Regardless of the type of disenfranchisement that exists, the fact is that disenfranchisement is real. Its effect that retains its victims is realistic. The effect of disenfranchisement can be viewed everyday in our abject impoverished schools, neighborhoods and communities. Researchers show that this problem, though not deliberate, has not gone unnoticed. Every year, policymakers, legislators (local, state and federal) parents, teachers and community advocates continue the struggle to improve the life chances, expectancy and quality of life for the disadvantaged. Ironically, after roughly forty years of requests (since the passage of the 1968 Civil Rights Bill), it could be inferred that economic, education, and social/political efforts to improve the conditions for African American males in this country have been non-impactive.

The argument for accepting the three types of disenfranchisement is spawned from the belief that it first must be identified before it can be defined and addressed. Research has revealed many truths to the existence of disenfranchisement. Nonetheless, despite the evidence of truth, one must still be willing to acknowledge it.

The following points were inferred, as a result of the research:

1. Racism is alive and well in America today.
2. There exists a large gap in both educational and economic achievement between African Americans and their Caucasian counterparts.
3. Everyday, more African American males lose their right to vote as a result of being victims of their environment.

CHAPTER 4

Economic Disenfranchisement

I remember being in the bathtub, and my grandmother and grandfather were talking about some incident that had been unfair and was racial in nature. They were talking about work and accomplishing things and how racism was getting in the way of that. And they looked at me and said, "Well maybe it will be different for him."

I couldn't have been more than about six years old. One of them, I can't remember whether it was my grandfather or my grandmother, said to me, "Well, is it going to be any different for you?"

And as I was climbing out of the tub and they were putting a towel around me, I looked up and said, "Yeah, cause why should white guys have all the fun?"

Reginald Lewis
Why Should White Guys Have all the fun?
1995

Economic Disenfranchisement: The Welfare Paradigm

Economically enlightening parables such as, "A fool and his money are soon parted," is a message that should resonate from the souls of previous generations. Parables of this kind, which instructed baby boomers and generation x-ers on the fundamentals of financial management, have now gone ignored. With a number of families living below the poverty level, and the sluggish economy awaiting a defibrillation shock, original American economists, like Adam Smith, have prolifically stated that our nation's economy will always correct itself (Smith, 1880). Despite this belief, America must now revisit a part of the welfare paradigm, which inevitably grows larger, with each passing generation of unchallenged, inequitable policies that disenfranchise African Americans.

In researching economic disenfranchisement, its blatant existence was found in the economically depressed regions of Memphis, Tennessee (i.e., census tracts with macroeconomic indicators of poverty such as: high unemployment rate, subsidized government transfers to the impoverished and other socioeconomic indicators). Reed (2003) paraphrases economic disenfranchisement as the lack of legitimate dollars made, spent and invested for the advancement of self, family and community. Macleod (1987) states that economic disenfranchisement is a continual, regressive slump, where access to financial resources are considerably limited and/or scarce (p. 19).

West (1993) highlights that the continuing paradigm of our nation's economic shortcomings (e.g., recessions, lack of economic stimulace policies for the indigent) has aided in the heightening of economic disenfranchisement of African Americans. Specifically, this problem is felt by African American men, who cannot establish themselves in a socially-traditional role, such as the head-of-household or "breadwinner." West (1993, p. xvi) continues, in this vein, by pointing out that "Wealth inequality tips the balance against fair opportunity in education, employment, and other crucial life chances. Corporate power . . . lessens the abilities of citizens and workers to have a meaningful voice in shaping their destiny."

West's (1993) comment introduces the problem that fuels economic disenfranchisement in the African American community—achievement gaps between disenfranchised African American men and their Caucasian counterparts. This discrepancy has been continually studied and revered by some as the single, most devastating issue that perpetuates economic hardship and disenfranchisement among African Americans, in urban areas. West's identification of the paradox (i.e., economic achievement gap) is also identified by the Urban League's study on Black America (2001). The Urban League highlighted multiple economic gaps between African Americans and their Caucasian and Hispanic counterparts. Specific economic gaps included home ownership, credit worthiness, living in abject poverty and employment.

A significant statistic highlighted that, "While black joblessness declined, (between 1985-2000) black unemployment rates still remained twice that of whites, and the black-white family income gap narrowed only slightly" (Daniels, 2001, p. 19). Despite the improved initiatives offered by certain economic reforms, (e.g., FHA home-buying incentives) there is still no significant increase in the number of African American men, 18 to 35, benefiting from them. Moreover, The Urban League's study also provided that there is a lack of economic institutions that communicate the benefits and incentives of economic policies, such as tax deductions, increased tax returns and equity (2001).

Policymakers sometimes develop economic reform for disenfranchised African Americans based on the perceptions of co-dependent behavior exemplified by welfare recipients (Mink, 1999). In the recent past, both the federal government and some states (e.g., Tennessee) have decreased funding for programs that have economically benefited disenfranchised African Americans. Examples of such program cuts can be witnessed in both the dollars earmarked for federal welfare programs and state medical insurance programs, like Tenncare, which accounted for roughly one billion dollars of the State's 2003-2004 fiscal year budget. Cornell West (1993) discusses decreases in funding to programs designed to supplement the incomes and services to disenfranchised African Americans.

In some disenfranchised African American communities, dependency on the federal welfare system is used as a crutch for sustaining life (Billson & Major, 1992). West (1993) contends that one of the reasons for abject poverty/welfare in disenfranchised African American communities can be attributed to racial bias in the job market. Although this supports the correlation between disenfranchisement and racism; conversely, others believe that, "... there is little evidence that racial bias makes Blacks poor, because it does not keep them out of all employment, although it may impede their advance into middle-class positions" (Hall, Kagan, & Zigler, 1996, p. 60).

Racism produces economic disenfranchisement, whether through unemployment, underemployment or the inability to create wealth (i.e., through the formulation of a business). Consequentially, low socioeconomic status is a derived indicator of disenfranchisement (Barton & Pillai, 1997). The overall problem in economically disenfranchised African American communities is not the fact that there is no employment, but, simply, that there is not enough legitimate output of capital to sustain an average quality of life (Goldratt & Cox, 1984). These scenarios, found in African American ghettos across the country, encourage the manifestation of crime and deviant behavior exemplified in many forms, such as drug use and gang violence (Evans, 2002).

Gwendolyn Mink (1999) shares a similar position on the effect of economic disenfranchisement toward African Americans. She states that, "The experience of racial oppression, the legacy of black struggles, and the capacity to survive in two contradictory worlds at the same time has left Blacks with a unique angle of vision on self, community, and society" (p. 230). Mink's point affords an opinion rarely provided by most researchers. Her dichotomous reference addresses black lifestyles of abject poverty. This entails the purchasing of superficial items that promote a pseudo-status of success amongst peers. This status allows economically disenfranchised Black men to identify success in themselves through the attainment of jewelry, luxury cars, and designer label clothing, all without acquiring a sound, personal economic infrastructure (i.e., homeownership, investments, generational wealth, etc.).

In many instances, African Americans, who have been economically disenfranchised, have had to find and/or create alternative economic means for survival. Consequentially, this, most times, leads to deviance from the law, incarceration and death. All of these problems have systematically perpetuated economic disenfranchisement by preventing some African Americans the opportunity of achieving a "normal life."

This "normal life" consists of a home, family and gainful employment. Today, it is still pursued by many disenfranchised African Americans, sometimes, at too great of a cost. Gwendolyn Mink, who has published her findings, regarding economically disenfranchised African Americans, now adds "For most of the twentieth century, white society did not treat middle-class Blacks as middle class. It denied them the privileges of class even when they could afford payment for them" (1999, p. 230).

Mink's quote exploits the fused concept of both systemic racism and the effect of economic disenfranchisement. Her quote exemplifies how systemic racism has been used by a racist, upper-class, majority to permanently disenfranchise African Americans economically (p. 230).

This system of economic racism has been perpetuated throughout the years, with such actions as denying African Americans privileges of homeownership, non glass-ceiling employment and adequate access to financial resources (e.g., banks and credit unions). Systemic racism is the catalyst for the perpetual welfare situation in disenfranchised African American communities. If not monitored and provided with intervention, quickly this lifestyle becomes permanent and irreversible.

This theory, coupled with Macleod's (1987) theory of low self-concept, are, perhaps, the two major reasons behind the economic disenfranchisement of African Americans today. Other researchers, who have stated that multiple factors (racism being one) contribute to the economic disenfranchisement of African American communities, also hypothesize the following:

1. There can be no single solution to the problem of welfare, and
2. Systemic racism found in America's economic system has created economic hardship for African Americans.

Yet another problem in the welfare paradigm is that both single mothers and their children are highly susceptible to poverty, regardless if they are on or off welfare (Garfinkel, Hochschild, & Mclanahan, 1996). Eventually, people are going to have to realize that the solution to welfare cannot be restricted to simply getting people off welfare because many single parents, who already work, do not earn sufficient income to maintain their basic needs budget standard (Garfinkel et al., 1996). Additionally, the characteristics of disenfranchisement preclude the general perceptions that policymakers associate with welfare and poverty. Some policymakers perceive poverty as a state-of-mind mentality that the poor conjure up from nowhere. Evidence of this mentality is shown in the statement, "Most low-skilled jobs also pay enough to get a family off welfare and out of poverty—provided the parents work the hours now typical of the society" (Hall et al., 1996, p. 60).

Contrarily, when several current welfare recipients read this statement, responses of anger and/or sarcasm always seemed to follow. When asked, the rhetorical response was mainly, "What are the work hours that are considered typical of society?" This response clarified the belief that those who function in society and those who dictate policy for society's inhabitants are grossly mismatched on their perceptions and beliefs about the economy's effect on those who are disenfranchised.

For many economically disenfranchised African Americans, the effect of poverty translates into an everyday life struggle, despite the opposing beliefs of some policymakers (Fuller, 2002). This hardship often creates a "survival of the fittest" mentality that, many times, svengalies young African-American men into a life of selling/using drugs and/or engaging in gang activity. This continued activity almost always results in incarceration and/or death. Moreover, this tragedy does not end here, but it continues to haunt the offspring of the disenfranchised. Again, this genocidal cycle results in the inevitable placement of incarceration and/or death. This cycle is also perpetuated by the other factors of disenfranchisement (i.e., educational and social/political). These factors work in concert to disassemble the possibility of hope by promoting a short-lived existence. This confusion leaves disenfranchised African American men with a narrow choice of money or life.

The characteristics of disenfranchisement (i.e., learned helplessness, loss of voting rights, etc.) are organized into three segments (i.e., economic, educational, and social/political) that prompt genocide in inner-city African American communities (West, 1993). This book has analyzed the possible causes of disenfranchisement and its potential effect on the African American community, specifically in African American men between the ages of 18 and 35. As this demographic was researched via surveys and focus group, the responses provided assisted with developing an understanding and identification of disenfranchisement and its characteristics.

CHAPTER 5

Sociopolitical Disenfranchisement

Nineteen fifty-four, when I was eighteen year-old is held to be a crucial turning point in the history of the African American for the U.S.A. as a whole—the year segregation was outlawed by the U.S. Supreme Court. It was also a crucial year for me because on June 18, 1954, I began serving a sentence in state prison for possession of marijuana . . . The controversy awakened me to my position in America and I began to form a concept of what it meant to be black in white America.

—**Eldridge Cleaver**
Soul on Ice

Social/Political Disenfranchisement

Thus far, each researcher on the topic of disenfranchisement has expressed either support or opposition (i.e., economic and educational disenfranchisement). Nonetheless, it is believed that social/political disenfranchisement is the most detrimental type of disenfranchisement hindering African Americans (Reed, 2003). This may largely be this way because of the Civil Rights movement that so greatly pushed for the equality of social/political rights in this country.

Reed (2003) discusses social/political disenfranchisement as the loss of the African American male's right to vote. Reed's definition is considered a form of social disenfranchisement because of the destructive impact felt throughout the African American community. This impact (i.e., voter disenfranchisement) prohibits millions of African American men from taking both a productive social and political stance from within their communities. "Justice Department statistics suggested that the African American community will perish based on the ongoing losses of young black [African American] men" (Reed, 2003, p. 1).

Evans (2002) suggested that the high number of African American men affected by voter disenfranchisement was a direct result of systemic racism. Evans elaborated her point in the following comment:

> You can't talk about racism without talking about the war on drugs . . . Virtually every drug war policy, from racial profiling to prosecutions to length of sentencing, are disproportionately carried out against people of color . . . people rarely make the connections. (p. 1)

And finally, social/political disenfranchisement can be identified as the loss or decline of rights and/or privileges of citizenship (Reed, 2003). This is characterized when disenfranchisement operates as an unforeseen force that prevents, disrupts and destroys life-changing opportunities for disadvantaged African Americans. Its lethal and genocidal effect is rapidly unraveling the ties of family, community and societal institutions (Muhammad, 2003).

At what point did our American society begin its fall from grace? Contenders against disenfranchisement, such as Dr. Martin Luther King, Jr. traveled the world, yet was assassinated in Memphis, TN. Most of the world remembered the cause of Civil Rights and, more than likely, believed that his assassination was largely, in relation to the African American struggle for racial equality. Nonetheless, we should remember that during the final years of Dr. King's life, his emphasis for equality transitioned from the struggle for racial equality, in this country, to a struggle for economic equitability, better known as the poor people's campaign.

As Dr. King held the attention of the entire world, he was able to use his charisma and influence to bring attention to the problems of racial and economic inequality for disenfranchised African Americans. As Dr. King would refer to America as being the richest country in the world, yet it treated its abject impoverished African Americans like second-class citizens, by having them languish in third-world living conditions; today, we can only speculate the ramifications of bringing about the truth, as only he did. On April 4, 1968, as the life of Dr. Martin Luther King was brought to a tragic end, sadly, so was the civil rights movement.

Interestingly, we can now see the damaging effects on the African American community, which lost both a substantial leader and message. Dr. King commanded the attention of the entire world by focusing on the inequities, which were unfairly thwarted upon African Americans.

As the lasting effects of poverty, non-education, the high rate of African American male imprisonment and other social-political indicators of disenfranchisement begin to profoundly present itself in urban, black communities; we must be about the business of resolving the issues which socially plague our schools, homes, and churches. These cornerstones of our society must be preserved, in order to save ourselves.

In looking toward our immediate past, we can pinpoint, exactly where the African American community has gone awry. Post the assassinations of Malcolm X and Dr. King, generation X-ers were produced. Post generation X, generation Y formulated a strong disconnect from the African American community through establishing a progression of apathetic mentalities and attitudes coupled with a coping mechanism of acceptance of social inequality. The identity of today's African American disenfranchised community includes the lack of economic, educational, and sociopolitical policies. These policies have removed parents from the equation of society. As a result, our disenfranchised, African American youth have now been charged with the responsibility of raising themselves. This is unnatural.

The social deviance displayed by many of our disenfranchised, African American youth (specifically men) comes directly as a result of the extraction of the African American man from the household and community. Of course, there is no public decree that positions Black men into prisons, prevents them from receiving education, or extracts them from their families. There are; however, policymakers that do not take into account the inadequate social construct and rigors of inner-city life, as well as the relentless odds that strongly prevent African American men from truly taking their rightful leadership positions as providers of households, educators, fathers to their children, and stronghold resources of their communities. In finding the resolve to these and other inequities, we, as a community in homeostasis, can begin to reconstruct the deconstruction of the black community.

CHAPTER 6

Research: Memphis, Tennessee

There are 3 kinds of lies: lies, damn lies, and statistics.
—Benjamin Disraeli

This chapter contains the findings from the analysis of the data collected. The findings presented both quantitative and qualitative data (i.e., surveys and interviews) on the existence of disenfranchisement in African American males, between the ages of 18 and 35, in Memphis, Tennessee. The data collected from the surveys were transferred to spreadsheets and analyzed using the Statistical Package for Social Sciences (SPSS) software program. The analysis resulted in a number of findings about the existence of disenfranchisement of African American males. The analysis was used to generate findings for the previous research questions. Qualitative data from participant interviews were also analyzed. This data generated a number of findings about the existence of disenfranchisement of African American males, between the ages of 18 and 35, in Memphis.

Approximately 384 (n=384) African American men were randomly selected to participate in the study. The two demographic variables studied included geographical location and age of participants. Participants for the study were selected from the north and south regions of the city of Memphis. The selection of these two regions was based on the census tracts that contained the highest concentration of impoverished African American males between the ages of 18 and 35. It was hypothesized that African

Americans residing in these areas would best exemplify the characteristics of disenfranchisement, such as: living in poverty (i.e., household income), felony arrest records, low educational attainment (at or below high school diploma level), low self-perception and unemployment. The south region of Memphis, Tennessee demonstrated the highest concentration of disenfranchised African American men. Findings about the regional breakdown of participants are presented in forthcoming data tables.

Sample

The population for this study consisted of African American males between the ages of 18 and 35. Currently, Memphis, Tennessee has a population of 650,100 (United States Census Bureau, 2000); 399,208 (61.41% of the total population) were African American. Furthermore, the 2000 United States Census Bureau report states that 131,279 of the men in Memphis are African American males over the age of 18.

The figure, 131,279 (N=131,279) was used to calculate an adequate sample size. Calculations determined that at a 95% confidence interval, a logical sample representative of the population would be approximately 384 (n=384) African American men, 18 years of age and older. This sample size allowed a random sample of approximately 192 respondents per segment of the city (i.e., North and South Memphis).

Qualitative focus group participants (n = 8) were randomly selected (pulled from a stack) from the list of surveyed respondents (n = 384). The eight randomly selected participants were contacted and asked to participate in a fishbowl style focus group, at a disclosed location. During the focus group session, an open interview was conducted and three questions (stemming from the three segments of disenfranchisement) were posed to participants. All responses were audio taped, printed and subsequently discussed in an effort to glean evidence of disenfranchisement and its related characteristics. Both findings on quantitative and qualitative data are discussed throughout the chapter.

The Survey Instrument

The following survey questions were critically developed and based on the ideology of anomie and apathy from previously field-tested questions:

Survey one (Quantitative/Descriptive):

1. I was assigned to a remedial or special education class in school. If yes: I feel that this assignment was fair or unfair.
2. I sometimes became frustrated with a subject in school: was the level of frustration strong enough to make me quit or weak, where it did not bother me.
3. I have participated in illegal drug sales in my community.
4. I have witnessed illegal drug sales in my community.
5. I vote.
6. I have failed a grade.
7. I have a criminal record. If yes, does my record include a felony charge?
8. I am unemployed.
9. I was held back a grade in school. If yes, was this action: fair or unfair.
10. My yearly income is below $20,000.
11. I received a high school diploma or GED.
12. I own a house.
13. I receive welfare benefits. If yes, it is impossible to live without this assistance.
14. I have thought about suicide.

Survey 2 (Qualitative):

1. Explain what it means to you to be educationally disenfranchised.
2. Explain what it means to you to be economically disenfranchised.
3. Explain what it means to you to be socially/politically disenfranchised.

Description of the Survey Instrument

Two types of research questions, each representing different measurement, were evident in this study. The first type of research question was demographic. These questions were identified in the first segment of the survey. They categorized the age and region of the city, where the respondent lived. The questions used in developing the first segment of the instrument (i.e., questions 1-14) were compiled from a list of previously field-tested sources (e.g., Fink, 2003a & Fink, 2003b). This practice eliminated researcher bias from the creation of the instrument. All questions, in the first section of the instrument, measured anomie in the sample population.

The second set of questions was used to generate qualitative data. These questions were used in the focus group (n = 8) segment of research. The purpose of these questions was to locate and/or match other possible indicators of disenfranchisement not previously discussed.

Content Validity and Internal Reliability

The use of statistical tests (alpha of .05) and multiple regression analysis were used in determining content validity of the survey. By adopting a pre-existing instrument, the researcher was able to avoid bias and show reliability.

Research Procedures

Both quantitative and qualitative methods were employed in this study. These methods were chosen because of their analytical ability to produce supportive data that contribute to both what researchers write about disenfranchisement and by evoking intangible phenomenon affiliated with disenfranchisement. Based on the surveys, respondents who exemplify a majority (70%) of the characteristics affiliated with disenfranchisement were analyzed and cross-referenced with other respondents possessing similar and/or exact survey response characteristics.

Eight (n = 8) surveyed respondents were randomly selected to participate in a fish bowl focus group discussion. Three questions, based on the three segments of disenfranchisement, were posed to the participants. All responses are listed and discussed in this chapter.

Procedures and Data Collection

A sample population of 384 (n = 384) participants were randomly selected from areas of Memphis, where research states disenfranchised, African Americans are likely to be found (i.e., streets, clubs, liquor stores, inner-city neighborhoods, etc.). Two areas of Memphis were identified through census tract research (i.e., North and South Memphis, see Figure 3) as being regions probable for finding disenfranchised African Americans. Poverty was used as the common denominator for the selection of specific census tracts in both the north and south regions of Memphis.

According to a study on poverty done by the Commercial Appeal Newspaper (1993), certain census tracts, in Memphis, have been identified as primary areas for poverty. With poverty being defined as income averaging at or below $20,000 annually, a plethora of census tracts in both North and South Memphis fit the research criteria. This finding, coupled with earlier research that suggested poverty as an indicator of disenfranchisement, served as a basis for selecting the following census tracts as desirable sites to conduct random surveys related to African American men over 18 affected by disenfranchisement:

> North Memphis: 6, 7, 8, 9, 20-25, 100, 101.10, 102.10 (13 areas)
> South Memphis: 47, 48, 49, 50, 51, 53, 56, 58, 60, 61, 65, 69, 78.10, 78.20 (14 areas)

> Grand Total = 27 census tracts

Research conducted in the aforementioned census tracts of North and South Memphis was thought to provide an indication of these areas being the primary sources for finding disenfranchised African Americans, specifically in men 18-35, who exemplify some of the following indicators/characteristics of disenfranchisement:

1. *Living in poverty (household income indicator)*
2. *Felony arrest records*
3. *Low educational attainment (at or below High School Diploma level)*
4. *Low self-perception*
5. *Unemployed*

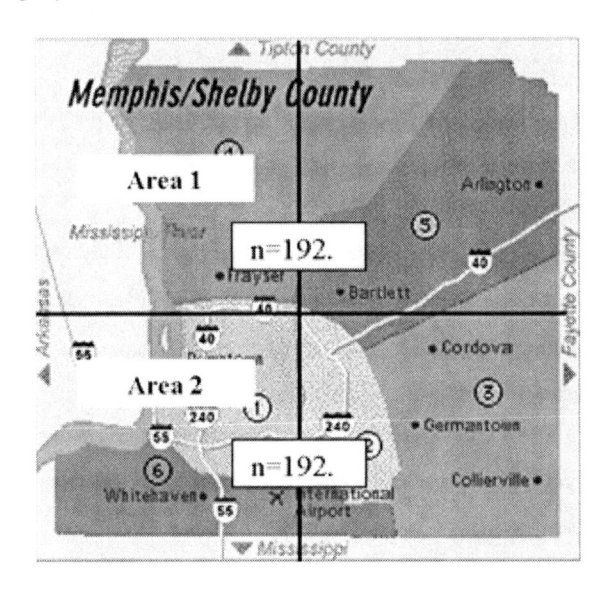

Figure 3. Areas of Memphis Surveyed (Commercial Appeal, 1993, p. A23)

The only pre-selection criteria was that participants be African American males and be between the ages of 18 and 35. Upon completion, surveys were collected and screened to determine if similarities of responses existed. Finally, all surveys were retained to denote trends and patterns. Of the 384 (n=384) randomly selected participants, 8 were randomly selected (blind random selection) for participation in a focus-group interview.

Selected respondents were contacted and invited to a disclosed location to participate in a focus group. Data from the surveys were collected and disaggregated using Multiple Regression and Analysis of Variance (ANOVA), using an alpha of .05. The data analysis attempted to discern the existence of a possible correlation between the representative sample population used in this study and the suggested characteristics of disenfranchisement (i.e., loss of voting rights, learned helplessness, and low self-perception).

The qualitative segment of this report acquired data by using both audio taped and written responses of the fishbowl-like focus group that began with approximately 4 participants sitting in a closed circle, facing one another, and an additional 4 participants standing in a closed circle, positioned around the seated circle of four. The seated, inner circle of participants was asked the three qualitative interview questions by the researcher. Their responses and dialogue were silently observed by the standing, outer circle participants.

Upon the completion of responses by the seated four, inner circle of participants, positions were switched again. This afforded the outer circle of four the opportunity to verbally respond to the three interview questions asked to the previous group. The outer circle of four (men standing) quietly observed the responses of the seated, inner-circle participants. This process continued, until the qualitative interview process was completed.

Statistical Analysis

All data from field research (i.e., surveys) was disaggregated in a criterion-referenced format, which produced individualized results. Surveys were analyzed for trend data, separated, counted, assigned numerical values and evaluated using SPSS. Implications of all findings are discussed in the forthcoming chapters.

Delimitations

Disenfranchisement is responsible for the shortened life expectancy of African Americans, specifically in men 18 to 35, who fall prey to its cycle.

Limitations

The limitations of the study are as follows:

1. *Characteristics of disenfranchisement, have not been previously defined.*
2. *Findings are limited to one city in a mid-southern, metropolitan area*

Data Analysis

This chapter identified various aspects of methodology: the research questions, data analysis and instruments. Statistical software disaggregated and compared variables for similarities, possible trends, statistical significance and possible correlations between the sample population and indicator(s) of disenfranchisement. With the results of this study, both a moral and civic duty must be exercised to inform our state, local and federal policymakers about our communities filled with socio/political, educational and economically disenfranchised African Americans, who, sometimes, see no possible way out of the desolation produced by policies, racism, anomie and apathy.

Table 1

Location of Participants

Area	F	%
North	170	44.3
South	214	55.7
Total	384	100

Two hundred-fourteen of the participants (55.7%) came from the south and 170 (44.3%) came from the north region of Memphis.

All responses were disaggregated in to four age categories. The first category was 18 to 21. The second category was 22 to 25. The third category was 26 to 30. The fourth category was 31 to 35. These categories were derived from an analysis of the age data. The distribution of participants' ages is presented in Tables 2 and 3.

Table 2

Distribution of Survey Responses by Age (A), Frequency (F) and Percentage (%)

A	F	%
18	36	9.4
19	29	7.6
20	16	4.2
21	18	4.7
22	18	4.7
23	19	4.9
24	27	7.0
25	33	8.6
26	9	2.3
27	14	3.6
28	18	4.7
29	22	5.7
30	34	8.9
31	13	3.4
32	15	3.9
33	11	2.9
34	18	4.7
35	34	8.9
Total	384	100

Table 3

Survey Responses Categorized by Age, Frequency (F) and Percentage (%)

Age Category	F	%
18-21	99	25.8
22-25	97	25.3
26-30	97	25.3
31-35	91	23.7
Total	384	100

Table 3 provides both frequency and percentage data, which show that 99 (25.8%) participants were between the ages of 18 and 21. Two age groups of participants, which accounted for 50.6% of responses, were between the age groups of 22 and 25 and 26 and 30. The remaining 91 participants (23.7%) were between the ages of 31 and 35.

Quantitative and Qualitative Findings

Quantitative data was disaggregated into a criterion-referenced format, which produced individualized results for the educational, economic and social/political characteristics of disenfranchisement. A relationship between disenfranchisement and anomie was also sought. Surveys were analyzed for trend data (i.e., affirmative answers to majority or all of questions). Quantitative data was used to analyze research questions one through four. In addition, qualitative data was collected from a focus group interview, which was conducted with 8 (n = 8), randomly selected survey participants.

Transcribed responses were categorized by research question and decoded. Interviews were decoded and responses were analyzed for themes and trends. Qualitative data was used to analyze research questions 1 through 3.

Answer to Research Questions

RQ1: What are the educational characteristics that lead to the disenfranchisement of African American males between the ages of 18 and 35?

Quantitative Findings

The quantitative findings for the educational characteristics of disenfranchisement are descriptive. Table 4 disaggregates the survey questions respective to measuring the indicators of educational disenfranchisement.

Table 4

Frequencies and Percentages: Educational Disenfranchisement Items (N = 384)

Item No.	Item	Yes f	Yes %	No f	No %	X^2
1.	Special Education/Remedial.	104	27.1	280	72.9	
1a.	Placement Fair/Unfair.	52	50.0	52	13.5	0.502
2.	Frustrated w/ a Subject in School.	242	63.0	142	37.0	
2a.	Feeling Strong/Weak.	135	55.3	109	28.4	5.773*
6.	Failed a Grade.	132	34.4	252	65.6	
9.	Held Back a Grade.	91	23.7	293	76.3	
9a.	Retention Fair/Unfair.	36	39.6	55	60.4	0.023
11.	Received a Diploma or GED.	288	75.0	96	25.0	

* $p <= .05$

There were a total of 384 participants in the study. On question 1, 104 (27.1%) responded yes and 280 (72.9%) responded no. An analysis of the 104 "yes responses" indicated that an equal number (52 and 52 or 50% and 50%) responded yes or no to question 1a. There was no significance difference in the responses of the two groups on question 1a. On question 2, 242 (63%) responded yes and 142 (37%) responded no. An analysis of the 242 "Yes" responses indicated that 135 (55.3%) responded Yes and 109 (28.4%) responded No on question 2a. There is a significance difference of 5.773 in the responses of the two groups on question 2a. On question 6, 132 (34.4%) responded Yes and 252 (65.6%) responded No. On question 9, 91 (23.7%) responded Yes and 293 (76.3%) responded No. An analysis of the 91 Yes responses on 9a indicated that 36 (39.6%) responded Yes and 55 (60.4%) responded No. There was no significance difference in the responses of the two groups on question 9a. On question 11, 288 (75%) responded yes and 96 (25%) responded no.

Qualitative Findings

The findings from the qualitative data are presented in table format. Additional comments were made by participants, which fully expose the phenomenon of disenfranchisement. Table 5 provides the distribution of responses for educational disenfranchisement.

Table 5

Participants' Responses about Educational Disenfranchisement

Question: Explain What It Means To You To Be Educationally Disenfranchised?

Theme	F	%
Evidence of disenfranchisement	3	37.5
Disregarded or no evidence of disenfranchisement	2	25.0
Experienced disenfranchisement earlier which was later recognized	3	37.5
Total	8	100

Three themes were identified. The "evidence of disenfranchisement" theme and "experienced disenfranchisement earlier which was later recognized" were both reported by 3 participants. The "disregarded or no evidence of disenfranchisement" theme was reported by 2 participants.

The findings are supported by the comments of participants. Participants in Group 1 are identified as G1A (Black, male, age19), G1B (Black male, age 22), G1C (Black male, age 35), and G1D (Black male, age 22). Participants in Group 2 are identified as G2A (Black male, age 27), G2B (Black male, age 25), G2C (Black male, age 34), and G2D (Black male, age 21). The full text of each response is given as follows:

G1A:

> Ahh . . . you know that's really difficult because ahh . . . what you don't know is what your life would've been like had you been enfranchised. The trip part is, ahh . . . you get the feeling that (expletive) was like this for everybody. I got pissed when I figured it out one day. It was like . . . that (expletive) teacher really screwed me, and I was too young and stupid to do anything about it (being assigned to remedial class). It was like a big lie. Back then, you used to trust your teachers, but lookin' at (expletive) now, I can't help but to keep thinkin' that I sho' would like to find that heifer, so that I could let her know that I know what she did to me.

G1B:

> I'm still not really sure about the question, but that write-up you gave us kinda helped. First of all, I think that being educationally disenfranchised means that you have been discriminated against during your time in school, right? Lookin' again at some of those questions, I would have to say that I agree with the one about being frustrated to the point of quitting the subject. I've been there lots of days. I remember that I would sometimes go to class, and my teacher would ask me questions and get mad when I didn't know the answers. I remember Miss

Karen was a good teacher, but she kinda got on my nerves with that not knowin' the answers mess. If I didn't know, then I just didn't know. Anyway, right, I remember that I was in remedial class from about the 3rd to the 8th grade. Then, when I made it to high school, I wasn't in remedial class anymore.

G1C:

In my case, y'know . . . the idea didn't hit me until I was in about 28. By that time, I knew that life wasn't fair for me because of race, but I wasn't gonna let conditions get the best of me. Instead, I took the road less traveled, humbled myself and did whatever it took. I answered yes on your survey about me being wrongly assigned to special education. When I was in school, I wasn't crazy. There were lots of other kids who were crazier than me. I never gave any teacher any problems! I just read slowly. And I still do!

G1D:

I don't think I suffer from this—I went to catholic school. I wasn't in remedial or special education classes. The only bad experiences that I had was not getting called on when I had my hand up. I don't really care about that anymore.

G2A:

I can remember, uh . . . going to class and gettin' mad with the teacher on several occasions, cause she said I gave up too easy. At first, I didn't pay it much attention, then it started botherin' me. I remember one time I said to the teacher maybe this is as smart as I am. I know now that she was really tryin' to help me, not hurt me.

G2B:

> I didn't enjoy elementary or middle school at all . . . Nah, I didn't like it. Teachers didn't teach me anything. They just hit us and yelled a lot. It wasn't until I got to high school that I was able to enjoy anything. I know that I was put in special education because I didn't like my homeroom teacher. She was always threatening me. My mom didn't really know a whole lot about school business. So, I think that she just went along with the teacher's request to put me in. When I got to special Ed, the work was too easy! I always got finished before everybody else, so she would let me play on the computer or help her (the teacher) when I got finished.

G2C:

> I don't really have a comment for this one.

G2D:

> I don't have much to say, but I know that I failed the 4th grade. My momma could've changed that, but I couldn't get her to come up to the school. I never did forget that.

RQ2: What are the economic characteristics of disenfranchisement in African American males between the ages of 18 and 35?

Quantitative Findings

The quantitative findings for the economic characteristics of disenfranchisement are descriptive. The findings for the economic characteristics of disenfranchisement are presented in Table 6. Significance is discussed.

Table 6

Frequencies and Percentages: Economic Disenfranchisement Items (N = 384)

Item No.	Item	Yes f	%	No f	%	X^2
8.	Unemployed.	122	31.8	262	68.2	
10.	Yearly Income Below $20, 000.	202	52.6	182	47.4	
12.	Own a House.	105	27.3	279	72.7	
13.	Receive Welfare Benefits . . .	40	10.4	344	89.6	
13a.	Impossible to Live Without.	30	75.0	10	2.6	3.617

*$p <= .05$

On question 8, 122 (31.8%) responded Yes and 262 (68.2%) responded No. On question 10, 202 (52.6%) responded Yes and 182 (47.4%) responded No. On question 12, 105 (27.3%) responded Yes and 279 (72.7%) responded No. On question 13, 40 (10.4%) responded yes and 344 (89.6%) responded no. An analysis of the 40 "Yes" responses indicated that 30 (75%) responded Yes and 10 (25%) responded No on question 13a. There was no significance difference in the responses of the two groups on question 13a.

Qualitative Findings

The findings from the qualitative data are presented in table format as well as through comments made by participants. Table 7 provides responses for economic disenfranchisement in the following:

Table 7

Participants' Responses about Economic Disenfranchisement

Question: Explain What It Means To You To Be Economically Disenfranchised?		
Theme	F	%
Evidence of disenfranchisement	3	37.5
Disregarded or no evidence of disenfranchisement	3	37.5
Experienced disenfranchisement earlier which was later recognized	2	25.0
Total	8	100

The "evidence of disenfranchisement" theme and "disregarded or no evidence of disenfranchisement" were both reported by 3 participants. Two participants reported the "experienced disenfranchisement earlier which was later recognized" theme. The findings are supported by the following comments of participants:

G1A:

> I know what I have, uh, seen in my hood. There is a lot of poverty. I know families that don't have money to buy enough food for the week . . . It's hard our here, yeah, cause I got a child to support. I tried to hustle legit, but eventually, I had to find me another hustle (people in circle begin to agree with him). Y'all know what I mean.

I look at it like this, if I'm a man, then I gotta do what I gotta do to get what I gotta get done . . . ya'll feel me? I don't know if it'll always be like this, but until somethin' comes along better, this is where I am.

G1B:

You can see it all around in the ghettos in this city. That's capitalism. The only thing we have forward to look to is the economy getting worse. I'm 22 years old, and I know I can't get a car . . . probably a house either. And another thing, you can't even get some jobs if your credit is messed up too bad. The only loans I have been able to get was some student loans . . . and sooner or later I gotta start payin' them back, if I can find a job.

G1C:

We all know that times are rough out here, but we have to arm ourselves with education. Instead of spending our money on trinkets and rims, we need to look at how we can begin to collectively invest our money. I was born poor, and I'm still poor today, but I at least keep the lights and phone on, and food in my fridge. My question deals with the black people who live in the ghettos and slums, but still can afford satellite television, Escalades and Bling-Bling jewelry. We have been taught to worship these small things that have no value, but other races are taught the importance of economic power. Another thing . . . why can't blacks own their own businesses in their hood? Why is it so important to live in an apartment? We need more community seminars on credit, home loans and spending habits. If we don't become educated we are doomed for a lifestyle of economic slavery.

G1D:

> Things are (expletive) up out here. I don't know if I'm economically disenfranchised cause I just wrote a business plan. I do need some money. If I can get someone to give me a business loan then I will be set. My parents always valued education. My Mama is a nurse, and my Dad's a mechanic. I'm not rich, but we've always had a house. Ahh, I always got what I wanted when I was young, but now it's my turn to make my way in the world.

G2A:

> I tried to get a house once. But I got turned down . . . Got denied on my application for a car too. So, I had to move in with my girl. She's got good credit. I work and help with the bills. I was able to save some money and buy a little cheap car at one of those U-tote places. I know I won't always be in this . . . uh, position.

G2B:

> I had to get a cosigner for anything that I've applied for. Like with my apartment. I'm a teacher, and it seems like I only make enough money to, uh . . . pay my rent, utilities, car note, insurance, buy food, pay my cable and then I'm broke. I ain't married and I don't have any kids.

G2C:

> I've been disenfranchised the same way we all probably have. I have probably seen a little more than some of you, so I'm lookin'

to get rich. The truth is that I have had money and I've been without it. I do what I can, when I can. I know that I don't like being without money, because I'm confined to one place. Think about those who live on fixed incomes and are confined to one place because they don't have enough money to do anything with. I've financed a house, but the finance charges are too damn high—the same with my car.

G2D:

Hungry all the time. Sick uh, not havin' money in your pocket. You see other people with stuff, and you go to wunderin' how they get that. Man, I done seen a whole lotta folk ridin' Mercedes Benzes in this city. You know they gotta be doin' somthin' they ain't got no business doin'. I'm through with school. You ain't gotta go to college to get paid. I know some uh my boys done got plenty cheese without going to school. Somebody just turned them on to some game. I believe it's just about being in the right place at the right time.

RQ3: What are the social/political characteristics of disenfranchisement in African American males between the ages of 18 and 35?

Quantitative Findings

The quantitative findings for the social/political characteristics of disenfranchisement are descriptive. The findings for the social/political characteristics of disenfranchisement are presented in Table 8. Significance is discussed.

Table 8

Frequencies and Percentages: Social/Political Disenfranchisement Items (*N* = 384)

Item No.	Item	Yes f	%	No f	%	X^2
3.	Participated Illegal Drug Sales.	96	25.0	288	75.0	
4.	Witnessed Illegal Drug Sales.	265	69.0	119	31.0	
5.	Vote.	241	62.8	143	37.2	
7.	Have a Criminal Record.	87	22.7	296	77.1	
7a.	Includes Felony Charge.	57	65.5	30	34.5	0.023
14.	Thought about Suicide.	63	16.4	321	83.6	

* $p <= .05$

On question 3, 96 (25%) responded Yes and 288 (75%) responded No. On question 4, 265 (69%) responded Yes and 119 (31%) responded No. On question 5, 241 (62.8%) responded Yes and 143 (37.2%) responded No. On question 7, 87 (22.7%) responded Yes and 296 (77.1%) responded No. An analysis of the 87 "Yes responses" indicated that 57 (65.5%) responded Yes and 30 (34.5%) responded No. There was no significance difference in the responses of the two groups on question 7a. On question 14, 63 (16.4%) responded Yes and 321 (83.6%) responded No.

Qualitative Findings

The findings from the qualitative data are presented in table format as well as through comments made by participants. Table 9 illustrates the qualitative distribution of responses for social/political disenfranchisement. Comments from participants follow the table.

Table 9

Participants' Responses about Social/Political Disenfranchisement

Question: Explain What It Means To You To Be Socially/Politically Disenfranchised?

Theme	F	%
Evidence of disenfranchisement	1	12.5
Disregarded or no evidence of disenfranchisement	4	50.0
Experienced disenfranchisement earlier which was later recognized	3	37.5
Total	8	100

One participant reported an "evidence of disenfranchisement" theme. Four participants reported a "disregarded or no evidence of disenfranchisement" theme. Three participants reported a "experienced disenfranchisement earlier which was later recognized" theme. The findings are supported by the comments of participants.

G1A:

> I know I haven't registered to vote yet. I listen to the old people in my hood. They be sayin' that it don't matter if you vote or not cause the white folk do what they wanna do anyway. Bush did what he wanted to do in the last election—he stole the white house.

G1B:

> I can't vote, and, uh . . . y'all know why. But you know the funny thing? I can run for office.

G1D:

> Yeah, he did steal the white house but that was only because we (blacks) didn't get out to the polls and vote. Imagine, If Gore had of won Tennessee; he'd be in the white house now. I know we didn't have a lot a problems when Clinton was in office. Can't he run again?

G1C:

> No, he can't run again—you only get two terms. But I tell you what we need to do, we need to get together and get this man out of office. We need to elect someone who has our concerns at heart. If you don't vote, you can't complain.

G2A:

> I haven't always voted, but I will vote in the next election.

G2B:

> I remember when I first voted when I was 18—I really felt like I had done something. I don't understand folks that don't vote. People fought and died over that. I've never sold drugs, but I've seen it sold in my community. If we want some of that to change, we're going to have to vote and understand what good political relationships are all about.

G2C:

> When I voted in the last election . . . I had the white people at the polls tell me that I wasn't in the system. I had my identification and my voter registration card, but they still wouldn't let me vote. I went in at two pm and did not get a chance to vote until about 8:30 that night—and that's only because I remained persistent. I wouldn't leave that place, until they let me vote. What's really sad is that the voting rights for African Americans are up in 2008. It will have to be signed off by congress again. If we don't become politically savvy and vote in large numbers, we just might go back to the way things were in the 1960s.

G2D

> I lost my right to vote like ol' boy. I see how it's important now.

RQ4: What is the relationship between the demographic variables, educational, economic, and social/political characteristics of disenfranchisement for African American males between the ages of 18 and 35 and anomie?

Quantitative Findings

The quantitative findings for the relationship between the demographic variables, characteristics of disenfranchisement and anomie are presented in Table 10. According to Durkheim (1933), anomie exists when social and/or moral norms are confused, unclear, or simply not present. The anomic condition can lead to deviant behavior (Durkheim, 1933).

Any findings regarding the relationship of disenfranchisement are contained in Table 10. The sections of the table highlight the demographic variables and each of the characteristics of disenfranchisement that were measured. A multiple regression analysis was used to establish a correlation between the variables, if any existed.

Table 10

All Demographic/Disenfranchisement Predictors Regressed on Anomie Mean

Item Type	Item	B	SE B	Beta	t
DM	Age.	0.004	0.006	0.035	0.699
DM	Location.	0.011	0.024	0.019	0.464
ED	Special Ed/Remedial Class.	0.387	0.075	0.245	5.130
ED	Frustrated w/School Subject.	0.147	0.065	0.102	2.216
ED	Failed a Grade.	0.002	0.081	0.001	0.020
ED	Held Back a Grade.	-0.091	0.088	-0.056	-1.035
ED	Received Diploma/GED.	-0.235	0.077	-0.146	-3.047
EC	Unemployed.	0.061	0.075	0.041	0.970
EC	Income Below $20,000.	0.067	0.069	0.048	0.970
EC	Own Home.	-0.171	0.080	-0.110	-2.126
EC	On Welfare.	-0.098	0.104	-0.043	-0.943
SO	Participated Drug Sales.	0.162	0.080	0.101	2.025
SO	Witnessed Drug Sales.	-0.012	0.068	-0.008	-0.176
SO	Vote.	-0.175	0.069	-0.122	-2.556
SO	Have Criminal Record.	0.196	0.085	0.118	2.301
SO	Thought about Suicide.	0.344	0.083	0.183	4.129

Note 1: DM = demographic predictor, ED = educational predictor, EC = economic predictor, SO social/political predictor.
Note 2: * $p >= .05$, ** $p <= .01$.

A *T-test* was used to establish significance. Findings indicate that the mean score between groups are large enough to be considered significant, or meaningful. There are several significance findings in the table. The demographic variables of age and location are not significant predicators of anomie. The educational characteristics of "Failed a Grade" and "Held Back a Grade" are not predicators of anomie. The educational characteristics of "Special Ed/Remedial Class", Frustrated w/School Subject", and "Received Diploma/GED", however, are significant predicators of anomie. The economic characteristics of "Unemployed" and "Income Below $20,000" are not significant indicators of anomie. The economic characteristics of "Own Home" and "On Welfare", however, are significant predicators of anomie. The social/political characteristic of "Witnessed Drug Sales" is not a significant indicator of anomie. The social/political characteristics of "Participated in Drug Sales", "Vote", "Have Criminal Record," and "Thought about Suicide" are significant indicators of anomie.

CHAPTER 7

Anomie and Apathy: Perceptions of Invisibility

> *I have also been called one thing and then another while no one really wished to hear what I called myself. So after years of trying to adapt the opinions of others, I finally rebelled. I am an invisible man.*
>
> **—Ralph Ellison**
> **Invisible Man**

The relationships between both anomie/apathy and the characteristics of disenfranchisement were examined. Descriptions of how anomie and apathy relate to disenfranchisement of African Americans, specifically male youth, have been thoroughly investigated. This further discussion and relevance of anomie and apathy, due to disenfranchisement, forces us to, more closely, analyze how disenfranchisement deconstructs our society.

Once disenfranchised, an individual accepts the scenario of life as is. There is little hope for empowerment or productive change. This is anomie/apathy. The sadness is that this depiction of our society is the harsh reality that many of our nation's citizens are faced with everyday. This disempowerment coaxes its disenfranchised host to believe that nothing will ever improve (e.g., life, money issues, and politics).

Upon the complete acceptance of apathy, disenfranchised, young African Americans are now demonstrating their non-conformity and non-adherence to laws through their consistent infractions, vicious murders, (drug and gang related) and statistically-high levels of incarceration rates, which are exemplified in every major city.

As apathetic, disenfranchised African American men, who may have once been perceived as silent and compliant to certain inequitable laws, policies and practices; are now, no longer reluctant to engage the consequences of their anti-social behavior. Although characterized as thugs, punks, and delinquents, the mentality is now, at least, they are no longer invisible.

Demographic Variables

Participants from various regions of Memphis were measured for anomie and apathy. Both the sample size and location for the study were randomly selected and followed a detailed methodology to yield a fair representation of the city's population. The age of participants was between 18 and 35. Consequentially, participants' ages were subdivided into four categories (i.e., 18-21; 22-25; 26-29; and 30-35) where the majority of participants selected proved to be between the ages of 22-25 and 26-30.

Research Question #1

What are the educational characteristics that lead to the disenfranchisement of African American males between the ages of 18 and 35?

Kozol (1991) implies that educational disenfranchisement is the lack of investment into human capital to make learning and instruction significant/beneficial for disadvantaged youth. The quantitative and qualitative findings indicated that some African American males, between the ages of 18 and 35, perceive themselves as educationally disenfranchised in the city of Memphis, Tennessee. The findings from survey question 2a indicated a significance difference (5.773) between participants who had "a strong feeling of frustration with school or a subject in school" and those who had "a weak feeling of frustration with school or a subject in school." In addition, 37.5% of the participants responded to the "evidence of disenfranchisement and experienced disenfranchisement earlier which was later recognized" as indicators of educational disenfranchisement.

Participants' perceptions of disenfranchisement generated numerous comments that described the impact of educational disenfranchisement experienced. In many instances, participants were fully aware of the negative impact that educational disenfranchisement has had on their lives. Participants also had a sense of what it meant to be educationally disenfranchised. All participants expressed regard of not attaining a better education. They also understood the relevance between educational, economic and social/political disfranchisement.

Research Question #2

What are the economic characteristics of disenfranchisement in African Americans, specifically males between the ages of 18 and 35?

Reed (2003) implies that economic disenfranchisement is the lack of legitimate dollars made, spent and invested by African American males for the advancement of self, family and community. According to Macleod (1987), economic disenfranchisement is a continually regressive slump, where access to financial resources are considerably limited and/or scarce (p. 19). There were significance findings from the multiple regression analysis of economic disenfranchisement. There were also findings from the qualitative data. Analysis of these findings indicated that some African American men, between the ages of 18 and 35, do perceive themselves as economically disenfranchised. In particular, 37.5% of the focus group responded to the "evidence of disenfranchisement," and 25% responded to the "experienced disenfranchisement earlier which was later recognized."

The findings suggest that some African Americans perceive themselves as being economically disenfranchised in the city of Memphis. Participants' perceptions of disenfranchisement generated descriptive comments that highlighted the impact of economic disenfranchisement experienced. The lack of economic means has had an impact on the quality of life of African American men, between the ages of 18 and 35, in the city of Memphis. Disenfranchised African Americans are continually compromised in their ability to acquire credit, attain an education, or even to marry. Ultimately, economic disenfranchisement jeopardizes the quality of life, life chances and expectancy of African American men.

Research Question #3

What are the social/political characteristics of disenfranchisement in African Americans, specifically males between the ages of 18 and 35?

Reed (2003) indicates that social/political disenfranchisement is the loss or decline of rights and/or privileges of citizenship such as, our democratic right to vote (this is also known as civil death). There were significant findings from the multiple regression analysis on the social/political disenfranchisement of African American males between the ages of 18 and 35. There were, also, findings from the qualitative data. An analysis of the qualitative data revealed that some African American males perceive themselves as social/politically disenfranchised in the city of Memphis, Tennessee. In particular, 12.5% of participants responded to the "evidence of disenfranchisement" and 37.5% responded to the "experienced disenfranchisement earlier which was later recognized."

The findings suggest that some African Americans perceive themselves as being socially/politically disenfranchised in the city of Memphis. Participants' perceptions of disenfranchisement generated numerous comments that described the impact of the social/political disenfranchisement experience. A total of 50% of the participants in the focus group perceived that African

The framework of disenfranchisement illustrates the vicious cycle, in which many African Americans, specifically men, are born. As with all cycles, there is a beginning and end. This cycle illustrates the star-crossed beginnings of African Americans, with the mentality of low self-esteem and concept. With the eradication of this mentality, life chances and expectancies of disenfranchised, black men will improve.

CHAPTER 8

The Civil Rights Era:
Adhering to the Messages from our Past

I truly believe that if ever a state social agency destroyed a family, it destroyed ours.

—Malcolm X
The Autobiography of Malcolm X

If we were truly smart, we, as a people, would take heed from sayings like, "Those who do not learn history, are doomed to repeat the mistakes of the past." Malcolm X left us messages warning us that this country would pay for the mistakes of racism. At some point, we must begin to look at the predictions made by predecessors who understood the future. Unfortunately, it is the emerging generations who are unable to, presently, see the deconstruction of the, already, disenfranchised black communities.

Eldridge Cleaver discussed the issues that were prevalent to black America, when he mentioned in his book, Soul on Ice, " . . . I began to form a concept of what it meant to be black in white America." Today, the question is, should black men still carry the stigma that Mr. Cleaver so fashioned from the recent past?

Malcolm X believed that black men are the most reviled and revered men on the face of planet. History supports this lesson. With approximately 314 years of the slave trade, and an additional 100 years of Jim Crowism, in this country; at some point, we must begin to realize that systematic racism in this country did not come to a screeching halt, with the assassination of Dr. Martin Luther King.

Indicators of the existence of disenfranchisement, should be prevalent to most Americans. Sadly, the reality is that either it is not recognized or it is ignored. Recent trends in policy suggest the latter. For instance, by dissecting the current trends of socioeconomic and educational policies in this country, we can actually witness the unraveling of the equitable policies that were implemented to "level the playing fields" for disenfranchised African Americans who would normally not be provided the opportunity to improve their life chances and/or expectancy.

Currently, some policies needing review include: Affirmative Action, No Child Left Behind, and the Welfare Reform Act. These policies demonstrate our country's shortcomings in servicing our less fortunate citizens, while simultaneously showing the ambiguity of the policymaking process. After slavery and Jim Crow, the Civil Rights Act came. At the end of the Civil Rights era, individuals felt that there was a sense of renewed hope. The expectation was that, perhaps, improved changes were on the horizon for African American men. Maybe, in fact, the "pioneers" such as: Fredrick Douglas, Asa Phillip Randolph, Henry Highland Garnett, Stokley Carmichael, H. Rap Brown, Fred Hampton, Bobby Seale, Malcolm X, Dr. Huey P. Newton, Dr. Alain Leroy Locke, Nelson Mandela, W.E.B. Dubois, Booker T. Washington and hundreds of unnamed others; would, somehow, change the negative perceptions, ideologies and unfair treatment of blacks in this country.

Every African American, in this country, should know the Declaration of Independence and the U.S. Constitution. These documents establish the precedence and foundation of inequality and disenfranchisement for African Americans. These policies, although not originally intended for African Americans, were eventually revised for inclusion. This occurred as a result of change agents who used the policymaking process, community and charisma to the advantage of the special interest. It is with aplomb that we must thank the great men and women who championed the plight of disenfranchisement through the fight to establish equitable policy. All policy being the precursor to law, we should turn to the resounding words of Dr. Martin Luther King, who once stated, "Injustice anywhere, is a threat to justice everywhere."

Looking back to the recent past, the Black Panther Party, who were once perceived by government to be the greatest threat to America, has now been recently viewed by scholars as an organization that contributed to lasting social change. Dr. Huey P. Newton, who served as the founding member of the Party, created a ten point plan, which, today, should be implemented by disenfranchised, African American neighborhoods and communities. This must happen in order to regain and preserve equilibrium for the continuation and safety of present and future generations.

Newton's ten-point plan sought to strengthen disenfranchised, black communities, as well as the country, by enacting the following:

1. *We want freedom. We want power to determine the destiny of our black and oppressed communities.*
2. *We want full employment for our people.*
3. *We want an end to the robbery by the capitalists of our black and oppressed communities.*
4. *We want decent housing, fit for the shelter of human beings.*
5. *We want decent education for our people that exposes the true nature of this decadent American society. We want education that teaches us our true history and our role in the present-day society.*
6. *We want completely free health care for all black and oppressed people.*
7. *We want an immediate end to police brutality and murder of black people other people of color all oppressed people inside the United States.*
8. *We want an immediate end to all wars of aggression.*
9. *We want freedom for all black and oppressed people now held in U.S. federal, State, county, city and military prisons and jails. We want trials by a jury of peers for all persons charged with so-called crimes under the laws of this country.*
10. *We want land, bread housing, education, clothing, justice, peace and people's community control of modern technology.*

When most people recall the turbulence of the 1960s, they, in fact, associate the Black Panther Party with terrorism. Although some may not have agreed with their methodology, the integrity of the ten-point plan is both assertive and equitable.

Simply, the devastating effects of disenfranchisement to urban, African American men have practically caused a disappearance of the black family, urban education and a disconnect of black churches with their surrounding community. With no immediate plan of action in sight, we should now begin to analyze how black communities were organized, before the introduction of drugs and the dissipation of the civil rights movement.

The ten-point plan is direct in what it asks. In reading it, disenfranchised African American men, any disenfranchised American, can relate to the deficiencies of community that prevent its citizens from obtaining the American Dream. To clarify, the American Dream consists of adequate housing, peacefulness of community and life, adequate compensation for the trade of goods and services, good personal health, quality education for our children and dignity and recognition from our fellow citizens; basically, " . . . life, liberty, and the pursuit of happiness."

CHAPTER 9

Looking Toward the Future:
Resolving the Issues of Disenfranchisement

> *The curse of poverty has no justification in our age. It is socially as cruel and blind as the practice of cannibalism at the dawn of civilization, when men ate each other because they had not yet learned to take food from the soil or to consume the abundant animal life around them. The time has come for us to civilize ourselves by the total, direct and immediate abolition of poverty.*
>
> —**Martin Luther King, Jr.,
> Where Do We Go from Here: Chaos or
> Community? 1967**

As the study of disenfranchisement has prompted this work, thus policy reform is the driving force behind the resolve. Abject poverty, in black communities, can be directly correlated to the disenfranchisement of African Americans. This work has thoroughly investigated both the methodology of intervention and prevention of disenfranchisement, and policy as the primary avenue for resolve.

The question of how to end disenfranchisement is as difficult a question to ask as how to end poverty or violence. In conclusion, the suggestions for resolve provided should not be perceived as the "be all, end all" to the surge of violence, death, and community degradation plaguing the inner cities of this country. Moreover, they should be perceived as preventative steps that should be strategically implemented in communities, where disenfranchisement is prevalent.

The empathetic reform of policies affecting disenfranchised African Americans is essential to bestow change. This change cannot and will not occur overnight, rather as surely as abject poverty, disenfranchisement, and community denigration has a beginning, thus it must have an end. And though it may never end completely, it can be controlled through policy—properly implemented.

A more detailed question that we, as community activists, should pose: is if African American neighborhoods will ever again reach community status, as they once did a few generations ago? Many African Americans, who were reared in inner-city communities, can recall the expectations of our predecessors. These parents, grandparents, friends-of-families and next-door neighbors all entirely contributed to the holistic raising of a child.

As these days have all but vanished, we must now look to our past to find exactly where the black community has gone wrong. Chaos has prevailed in many neighborhoods in the forms of high crime, secondary cohort dropout rates, high adolescent and teenage pregnancies, high rates of drug use and sales and a strong sense of nobodiness.

Recommendations

The following policy recommendations provide a real-world resolve for economic, educational, and socio-political disenfranchisement:

1. The appropriate policy makers in the various school districts, units of government, social organizations and the business sector should examine, identify and address factors that negatively impact the educational enfranchisement of African Americans, specifically men between the ages of 18 and 35, in both the city of Memphis, TN and abroad.

2. The appropriate policy makers in the various school districts, units of government, social organizations and the business sector should examine, identify and address those factors that negatively impact the economic enfranchisement of African Americans, specifically men between the ages of 18 and 35 in the city of Memphis, TN and abroad.
3. The appropriate policy makers in the various school districts, units of government, social organizations and the business sector should examine, identify and address those factors that negatively impact the social/political enfranchisement of African Americans, specifically men between the ages of 18 and 35 in the city of Memphis, TN and abroad.
4. The appropriate policy makers in the various school districts, units of government, social organizations and the business sector should examine and address the relationship between the educational, economic and socio-political disenfranchisement and anomie for disenfranchised African Americans, specifically men between the ages of 18 and 35.

Suggestions for Further Research

The following suggestions for future research are made:

1. Research to canonize the definitions used for educational, economic, and social/political disenfranchisement.
2. Research to clarify the definition used for anomie.
3. Similar research in other metropolitan areas with similar demographics as Memphis, TN.
4. Similar research on White, Asian American, Hispanic, and Native American males between the ages of 18 and 35.
5. Research on educational, economic, and social/political responses to the conditions of disenfranchisement.

6. Revised, Cycle of Disenfranchisement Schema. The schema is illustrated in Figure 4.
7. Extensive research on the effect of Disenfranchisement on African American Women.

Looking toward the future, there must be an implementation of policy and practicum to end the plague of disenfranchisement, and its disastrous effects on urban, African American communities. Change must be implemented in both a traditional and nontraditional fashion. This change must entail a more sensitive approach from policymakers, who produce policies that mainly effect the disenfranchised. Change must also come from the application side of the equation, where the rubber meets the road. There must be a revitalization of the civil rights movement that was prematurely halted. Only this time, the struggle must also address what African Americans have done to destroy community. African Americans must take charge of their urban communities, where the indicators of disenfranchisement are prominently displayed. These endeavors to recover from disenfranchisement will only be successful when community activists and policymakers learn to communicate and produce fair and equitable policies together.

With community being defined as people + activities, we must strive to re-engage the travesties of the inner-city. Activities that will prompt generational change to disenfranchised communities must include, but not be limited to, the following:

1. After-school academic programs
2. Parenting classes for adolescents, teens, and young adults
3. Athletic programs
4. College prepatory initiatives
5. Social action initiatives
6. Health awareness programs
7. Economic and financial education

8. Critical thinking exercises
9. Community service engagement
10. Civics education

Expectation of empathy in policymaking is only half of the equation for change. At some point, the disenfranchised, themselves, must begin to take responsibility for the change of their own situations. When this occurs, community begins to take responsibility for itself, and the disenfranchised can become enfranchised.

REFERENCES

Barton, T., & Pillai, V. K. (1997). *Welfare as we know it: a family-level analysis of AFDC receipt.* Lewiston, NY: Edwin Mellen Press.

Bender, D. L., & Leone, B. (1991). *Racism in America: opposing viewpoints.* San Diego: Greenhaven Press.

Berryhill, D. A. (2001). National study shows that charters motivate change in school districts. *Resource, 4,* 1-5.

Billson, J. M., & Major, R. (1992). *Cool Pose: the dilemmas of black manhood in America.* New York: Simon & Schuster.

Civil Rights Project, The. (2001). Harvard studies find inappropriate special educational placements continue to segregate and limit educational opportunities for minority students nationwide. Retrieved May 30, 2004 from http://www.charityadvantage.com.

Comer, J. P., & Poussaint, A. J. (1992). *Raising black children.* New York: Penguin Group.

Commercial Appeal, The. (1993, January). Census tract figures show wide income disparity. Retrieved from the Commercial Appeal Newspaper in Memphis, TN. A3, p. 10.

Cowan, K. T., & Manasevit, L. M. (2002). *The new title I: balancing flexibility with accountability.* Washington, DC: Thompson Publishing Corp.

Daniels, L. (2001). *The state of black America 2001.* New York: The National Urban League.

Davis, R. (2001). Interview with milton bradley of tennesseans for fair taxation.

Durkheim, Emile. 1933. The Division of Labor in Society Translated by George Simpson. New York: The Free Press.

Evans, D. (2002). Race and the drug war. Retrieved November 3, 2003 from http://www.alternet.org/story/14085

Fink, A. (2003a). *How to ask survey questions.* Thousand Oaks, CA: Sage Publications, Inc.

Fink, A. (2003b). *How to report on surveys.* Thousand Oaks, CA: Sage Publications, Inc.

Finnegan, W. (1998). *Cold new world: grown-up in a harder country.* New York: Random House.

Fuller, H. (1999). Transforming education in America. *The School Choice Advocate,* (Vol. 1, pp. 3-8.). Minnesota: The Free Press.

Garfinkel, I., Hochschild, J. L., & Mclanahan, S. S. (1996). *Social policies for children.* Washington, DC: The Brookings Institution.

Giddens, Anthony. 1972. Emile Durkheim: Selected Writings. London: Cambridge University Press.

GIS. (2001). The policy cycle. Retrieved November 2, 2003 from http://www.ces.ncsu.edu depts./design/research/WECO/policyGIS/cycle.html

Goldratt, E. M., & Cox, J. (1984). *The goal.* Great Barrington, MA: The North River Press.

Gordon, R., & Gordon, M. (1996). Learned helplessness and school failure. Retrieved November 3, 2003 from http://www.ldaca.org/gram/gordon.htm.

Hall, N. W., Kagan, S. L., & Zigler, E. F. (1996). *Children, families & government: preparing for the 21st century.* New York: Cambridge University Press.

Haskins, J. (1973). *Black manifesto for education.* New York: William Morrow & Company, Inc.

Jones, C. O. (1997). An introduction to the study of public policy. Massachusetts: International Thomson Publishing

Kozol, J. (1992). *Savage inequalities: children in America's schools*. Addison, TX: Harper Perennial.
Kunjufu, K. (1982). *Countering the conspiracy to destroy black boys*. St. Louis: Twenty-sixth Printing.
Kuykendall, C. (1991). Keynote address: The high road to life. Wholistic Institute, Atlanta, GA.
Ladner, M. (2004). Racial bias in pennsylvania special education. Retrieved May 30, 2004 from http://wwwCommonwealthFoundation.org
Macleod, J. (1987). *Ain't no makin' it: leveled aspirations in a low-income neighborhood*. Boulder, CO: Westview Press.
McCall, N. (1994). *Makes me wanna holler: A young black man in America*. New York: Vintage.
McWhirter, J. J., McWhirter, B. T., McWhirter, A. M., & McWhirter, E. H. (1993). *At-risk youth: A comprehensive response for counselors, teachers and human service professionals*. Pacific Grove, CA: Brooks/Cole Publishing.
Mink, G. (1999). *Whose welfare?* Ithaca, NY: Cornell University Press.
Muhammad, N. I. (2003, September). Back to failing schools: as the school system disintegrates, educators advocate better choice for teaching black children. *The final Call*: (pp. 6-7, 31.)
Neal, L. (2003). The effects of African American movement styles on teachers' perceptions and reactions. Retrieved May 30, 2004 from http://www.findarticles.com.
Owo, Y. (2004). African-Americans still face discrimination in schools. Retrieved May 30, 2004 from http://www.dailytexanonline.com
Popekewitz, T. S. (2000). *Educational knowledge: changing relationships between the state, civil society, and the educational community*. New York: State University of New York Press.
Queensland Policy Handbook. (2001). The policy cycle. Retrieved May 30, 2004 from http://www.premiers.qld.gov.au/governingqld/policy/cycle1_1.html

Reed, W. (2003). *Where's our talented tenth? over a million black men in prison.* Retrieved November 3, 2003 from http://www.nbfea.com/NEWS/news03/comments/Talent

Robinson, J. P., Shaver, P. R., & Wrightsman, L. S. (1991). *Measures of personality and social psychological attitudes.* San Diego, CA: Academic Press.

Schansberg, D. E. (1996). *Poor policy: how the government harms the poor.* Boulder Colorado: Westview Press.

Shakur, S. (1993). *Monster: The autobiography of an L.A. gang member.* New York: Penguin Books.

Shields, K. (1997). *The conflicts of learned helplessness in motivation.* Retrieved November 5, 2003 from http://ematusov.soe.udel.edu/final.paper.pub/_pwfsfp

Smith, A. (1880). *An inquiry into the nature and causes of the wealth of nations.* Oxford: Clarendon Press.

Tukufu, D. S. (1997). *A guide toward the successful development of african-american males.* Richmond Heights, OH: The Tukufu Group.

US Census 2000. (2000). Memphis, City Tennessee Statistics and Demographics. Retrieved January 1, 2003 from *http://www.memphis.areaconnect.com/statistics.html.*

West, C. (1993). *Race matters.* New York: Vintage Books.

Wynn, M. (1992). *Empowering african american males to succeed.* Pasadena, CA: Rising Sun Publishing.

WORKS CONSULTED

Anderson, W. (2002). Memphis African American survey results. Memphis, TN: The Anderson Group.

Appalachian Educational Laboratories (AEL). (2004). Interview on conducting Focus Groups.

Chiong, J. A. (1998). *Racial categorization of multiracial children in school.* Westport, CT: Bergin & Garvey.

Eaton, S. E., Orfield, G., & The Harvard Project on School Desegregation. (1996). *Dismantling desegregation: the quiet reversal of brown vs. board of education.* New York: The New Press.

Fife, B. L. (1992). *Desegregation in American schools: comparative intervention strategies.* New York: Praeger Publishers

Freedman, J. (1993). *From cradle to grave: the human face of poverty in America.* Atheneum, New York: Maxwell Macmillard.

NAACP. (2004). Home ownership initiative. Retrieved April 17, 2004 from http://www.detroitnaacp.org/economics /homeownership.asp.

National Center for Public Policy. (1994). Introduction to Project 21's 1994 Annual Report, Black America 1994: Changing Direction. Retrieved January 3, 2004 from http://www.national center.org/P21Intro94Rpt.html.

APPENDIX

Appendix A

Indicators (Problems) Caused by Disenfranchisement

The problems caused by disenfranchisement have been clearly outlined. According to Reed (2003), and other researchers, disenfranchised African Americans, specifically men, are identified by the following:

1. "The imprisonment of young black men . . ." (Reed, p. 3, 2003),
2. Loss of voting rights through felony arrest
3. Tolerance of "poor life" conditions (MacLeod, 1987)
4. High unemployment rate
5. Decimated economy
6. Apathetic attitude toward policy that promotes an improved quality of life (i.e., No Child Left Behind, Voting Rights Act, etc.)
7. Poverty level and schools receiving Title I funding as a possible correlation between African Americans and disenfranchisement
8. Academically low-performing schools (as identified by the No Child Left Behind Act) with high absenteeism/dropout rates immersed within disadvantaged, African-American communities
9. African-American communities with high reports of homicide, gang, and drug activity
10. Influx of African-American students wrongly assigned to special education

ACKNOWLEDGEMENTS

I would foremost like to thank all opposition that attempted to prevent this work from becoming a reality—a beacon of light. Social consciousness in the African-American community is prevalent. At some point, we must acknowledge our mistakes. Either you are a part of the problem, or you are a part of the solution.

The JAMAR Institute

www.thejamarinstitute.com

Dr. Ron Davis

Executive Director

Request for Consultation

I would like to request the services of the JAMAR Institute for one (or more) of the following. Please check all that apply:

__ School/district conference

__ Team/Athletic Consultation

__ Community presentation

__ Keynote presentation

__ Professional development

__ Other:

Thank you for selecting the JAMAR Institute for your consulting needs. Upon completion of this form, please return to the following address or email us at: *mail@thejamarinstitute.com*

The JAMAR Institute

P.O. Box 752663

Memphis, TN 38175

(901) 361-1596 ph.1

(901) 859-9774 ph. 2